Easy Piano

W9-AGW-820

Playing THE Blues

33 hot songs for Gettin' Good 'n' Low Down

This publication is not for sale in the E.C. and/or Australia or New Zealand.

ISBN 0-7935-5847-6

A JOINT PUBLICATION OF

MCA music publishing

A DIVISION OF MCA INC.
7777 W. BLUEMOUND RD. MILWAUKEE, WI 53213
AND

HAL•LEONARD® CORPORATION
7777 W. BLUEMOUND RD. P.O. BOX 13819 MILWAUKEE, WI 53213

© Copyright 1996 by MCA MUSIC PUBLISHING, A Division of MCA INC.
and HAL LEONARD CORPORATION
International Copyright Secured All Rights Reserved
MCA music publishing

For all works contained herein:
Unauthorized copying, arranging, adapting, recording or public performance is an infringement of copyright.
Infringers are liable under the law.

The Hottest Music of the '90s Is THE Blues

4 Baby, Won't You Please Come Home

7 Boogie Chillen No. 2

10 Boom Boom (Out Go the Lights)

13 Checkin' Up on My Baby

16 Chicago Blues

21 Crazy Blues

30 Diving Duck

26 Down Hearted Blues

37 Everyday (I Have the Blues)

42 Fine and Mellow

50 A Good Man Is Hard to Find

47 Heartbreak Hotel

54 Help Me

58 I'm a Man

61 In the Evening (When the Sun Goes Down)

64 It's a Low Down Dirty Shame

67 Mad About Him, Sad Without Him, How Can I Be Glad Without Him Blues

72 Mean Old World

78 Memphis Blues

84 Milk Cow Blues

75 Mule Kicking in My Stall

90 My Baby Left Me

92 Pinetop's Blues

100 Rock Me Baby

102 Saint James Infirmary

104 Smokestack Lightning

95 St. Louis Blues

106 Sugar Blues

109 Tain't Nobody's Biz-ness If I Do

118 The Thrill Is Gone

114 Tobacco Road

124 West End Blues

121 Why I Sing the Blues

BABY, WON'T YOU PLEASE COME HOME

Words and Music by CHARLES WARFIELD
and CLARENCE WILLIAMS

© Copyright 1919 by MCA MUSIC PUBLISHING, A Division of MCA INC. and GREAT STANDARDS MUSIC PUBLISHING COMPANY
Copyright Renewed
All Rights for GREAT STANDARDS MUSIC PUBLISHING COMPANY Administered by THE SONGWRITERS GUILD OF AMERICA
International Copyright Secured All Rights Reserved

MCA music publishing

A7 D7 Dm7 G7 C
graph you, ba - by, ask you won't you please come home. 'Cause

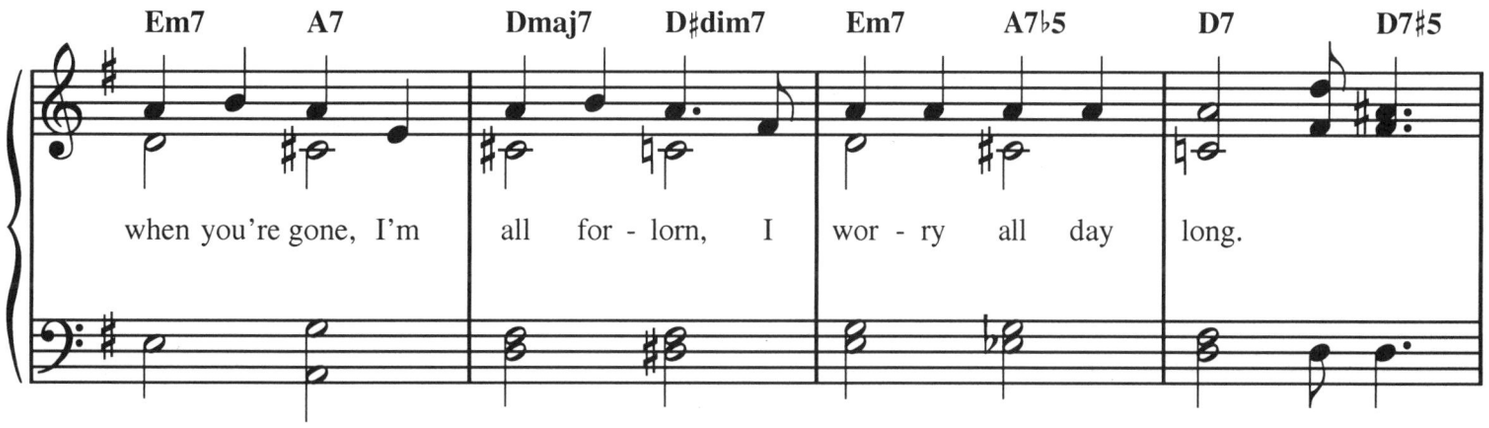
Em7 A7 Dmaj7 D♯dim7 Em7 A7♭5 D7 D7♯5
when you're gone, I'm all for - lorn, I wor - ry all day long.

G F♯m7 F7 E7 A7 Em7
Ba - by, won't you please come home, 'cause your mam-ma's all a -

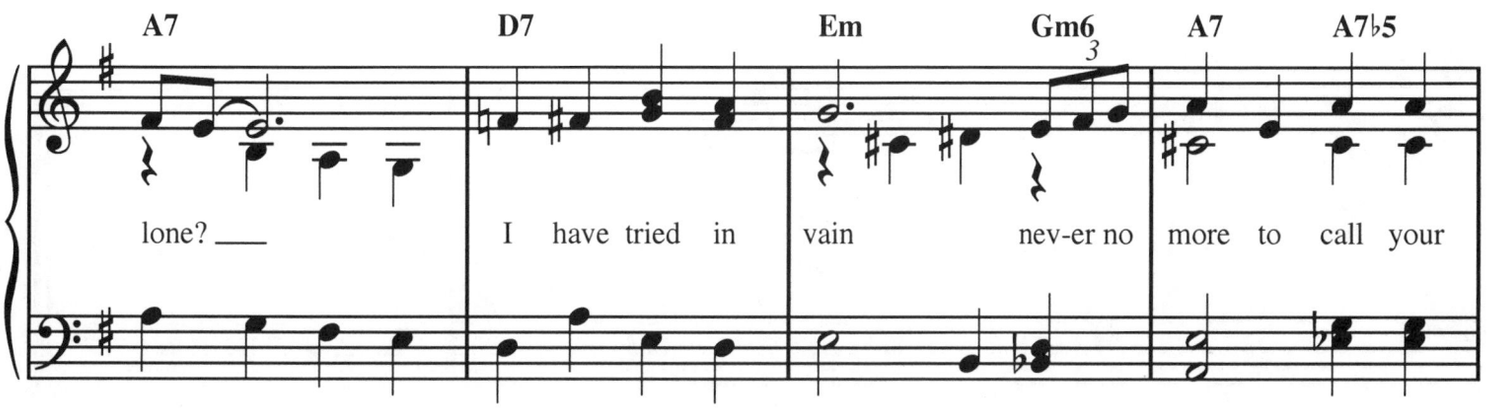
A7 D7 Em Gm6 A7 A7♭5
3
lone? ___ I have tried in vain nev-er no more to call your

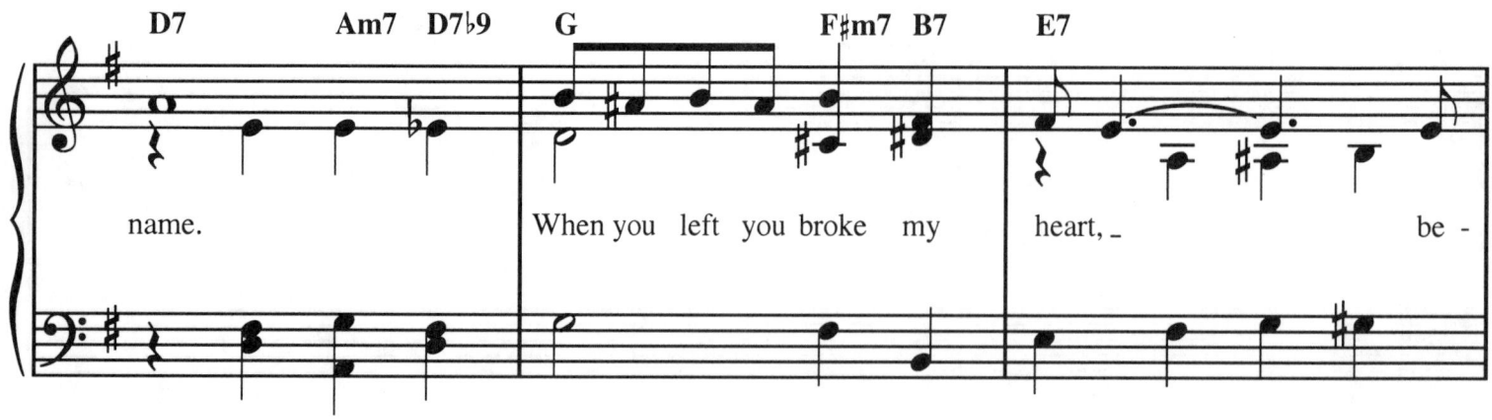
D7 Am7 D7♭9 G F♯m7 B7 E7
name. When you left you broke my heart, be -

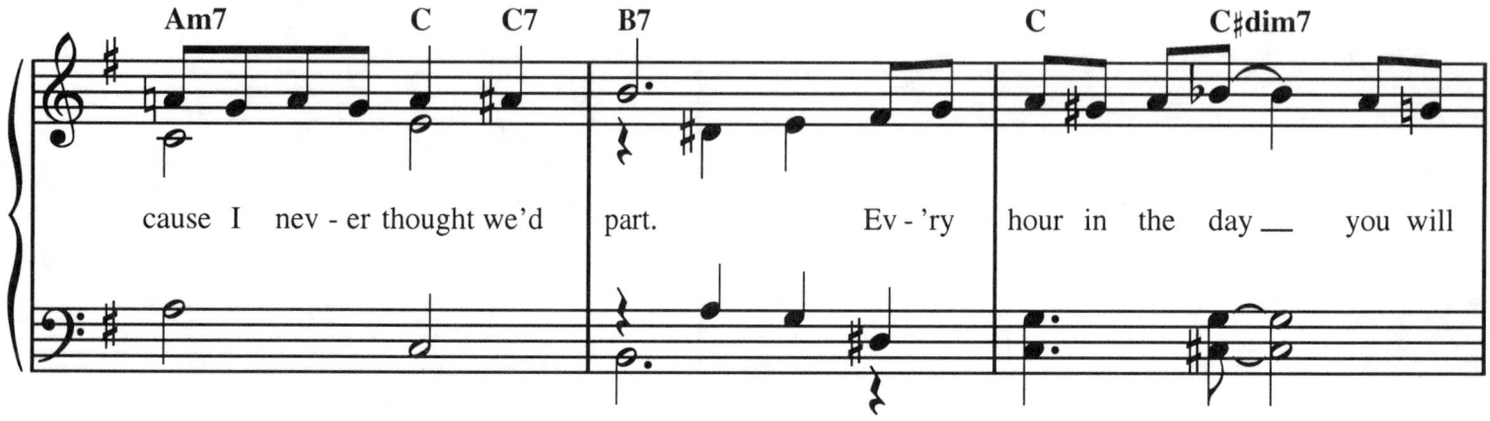
Am7 C C7 B7 C C♯dim7
cause I nev - er thought we'd part. Ev - 'ry hour in the day you will

1.
G B7 E7 A7 D7 G D7sus D7♯5
hear me say, ba - by, won't you please come home?

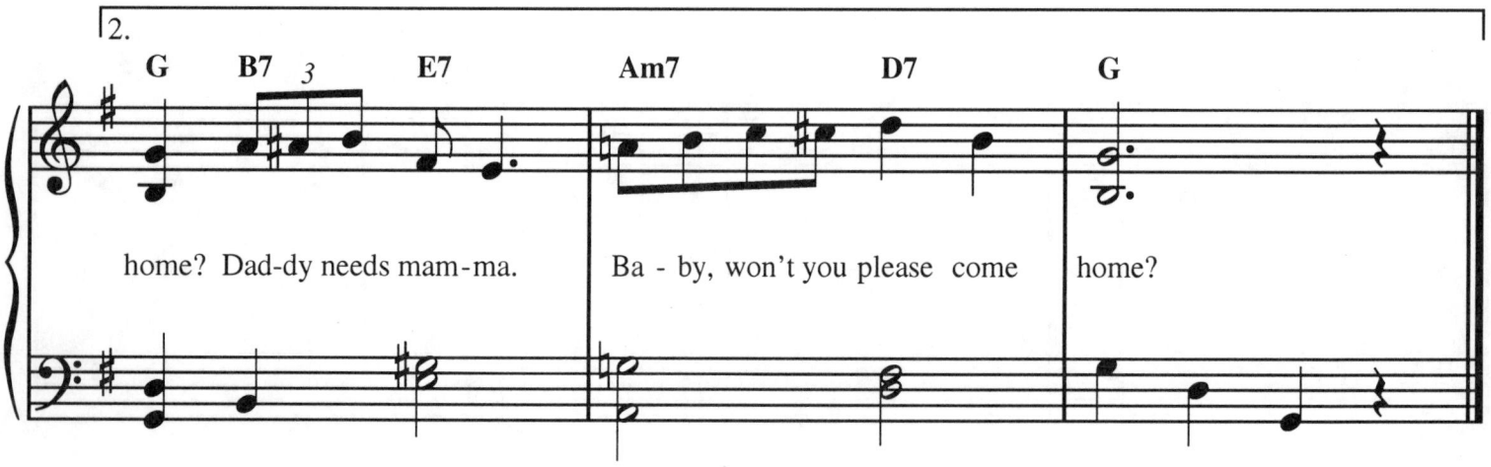
2.
G B7 3 E7 Am7 D7 G
home? Dad-dy needs mam-ma. Ba - by, won't you please come home?

BOOGIE CHILLEN NO. 2

Words and Music by JOHN LEE HOOKER
and BERNARD BESMAN

© 1970 ATV MUSIC CORP. and LA CIENEGA MUSIC COMPANY
All Rights Controlled and Administered by EMI BLACKWOOD MUSIC INC. under license from ATV MUSIC CORP.
All Rights Reserved Internaitonal Copyright Secured Used By Permission

G7
4
will be com-ing back. I'm a
D7
3
man now, ba - by, and I sure can have my fun.
G7
My ba - by got some-thin'
round like an ap - ple, shaped like a pear,

C7
sure now, babe. My ba - by got some - thin'.
G
My ba - by got some - thin'.
D7
My ba - by got some - thin',
G
Ab7 G
man, I sure do love.

BOOM BOOM

(Out Go The Lights)

By STAN LEWIS

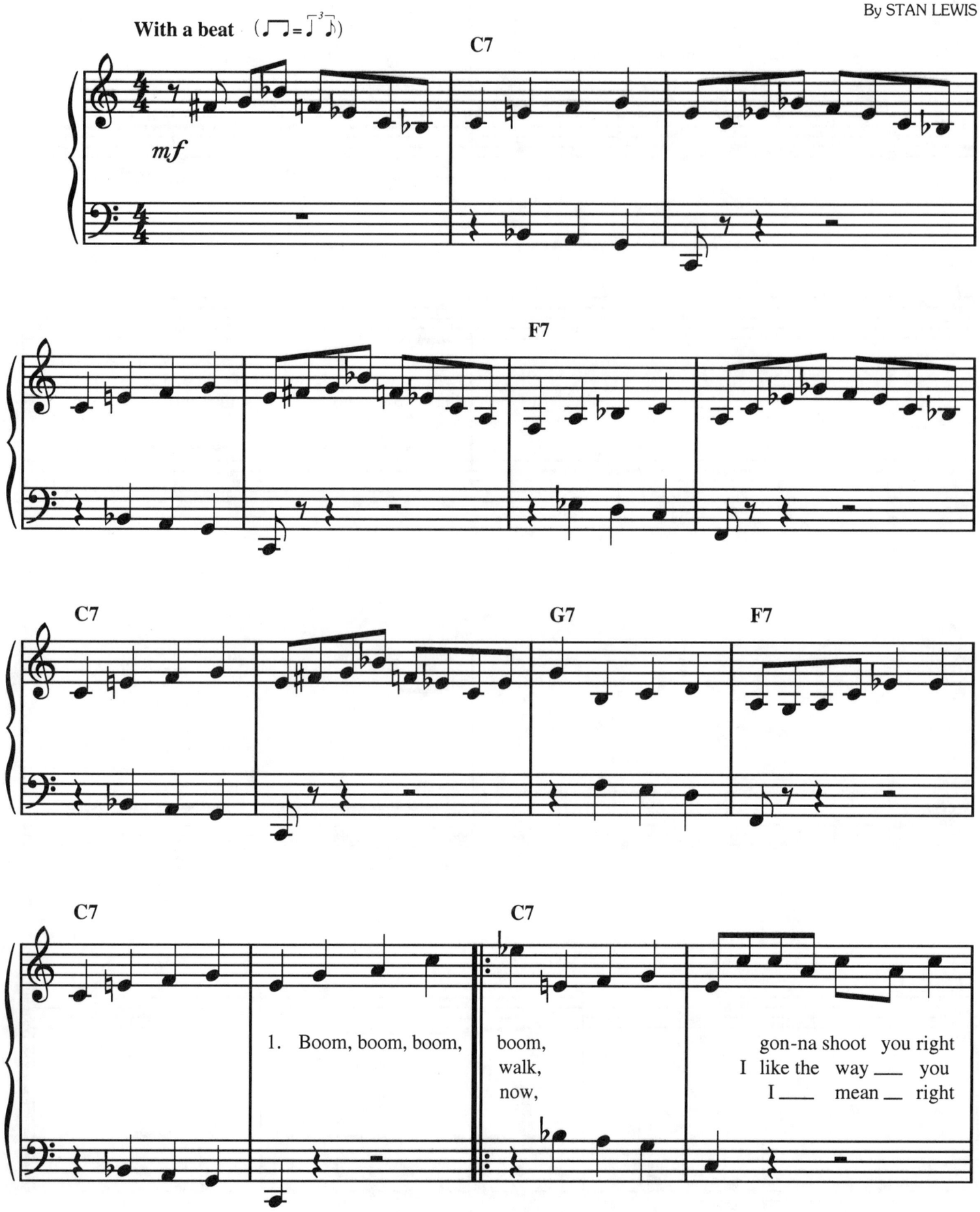

Copyright © 1957 (Renewed) by Arc Music Corp.
International Copyright Secured All Rights Reserved

F7
down. Take you in my arms,
talk when you walk that walk
now. I don't mean to - morrow,
C7
I'm in love with you. Love that is
and you talk that talk. You knock me
I ____ mean right now. Come on, come
G7 F7 C7
1., 2.
true, boom, boom, boom, boom. 2. I like the way you
out, boom, boom, boom, boom. 3. I need you right
on, boom, boom, boom, boom.
3.
C7
Come on, ___ and shake, shake it up,
(Group: Shake it, ba - by.)

F7
ba - by.
(Shake it
Come on ___ now,
ba - by.)
ba - by,
(Shake it,
C7
I don't mean
ba - by.)
may - be.
(Shake it,
You're driv - in' me
Come on, _____ come
ba - by.)
G7
cra - zy,
on, _____
(Shake it,
F7
come on, ___ come
all right, _ all
ba - by.)
1.
C7
on.
on.
(Shake it,
2.
C7
Come on ___ and
ba - by.)
right.
(Shake it,
C
ba - by.)

CHECKIN' UP ON MY BABY

By SONNY BOY WILLIAMSON

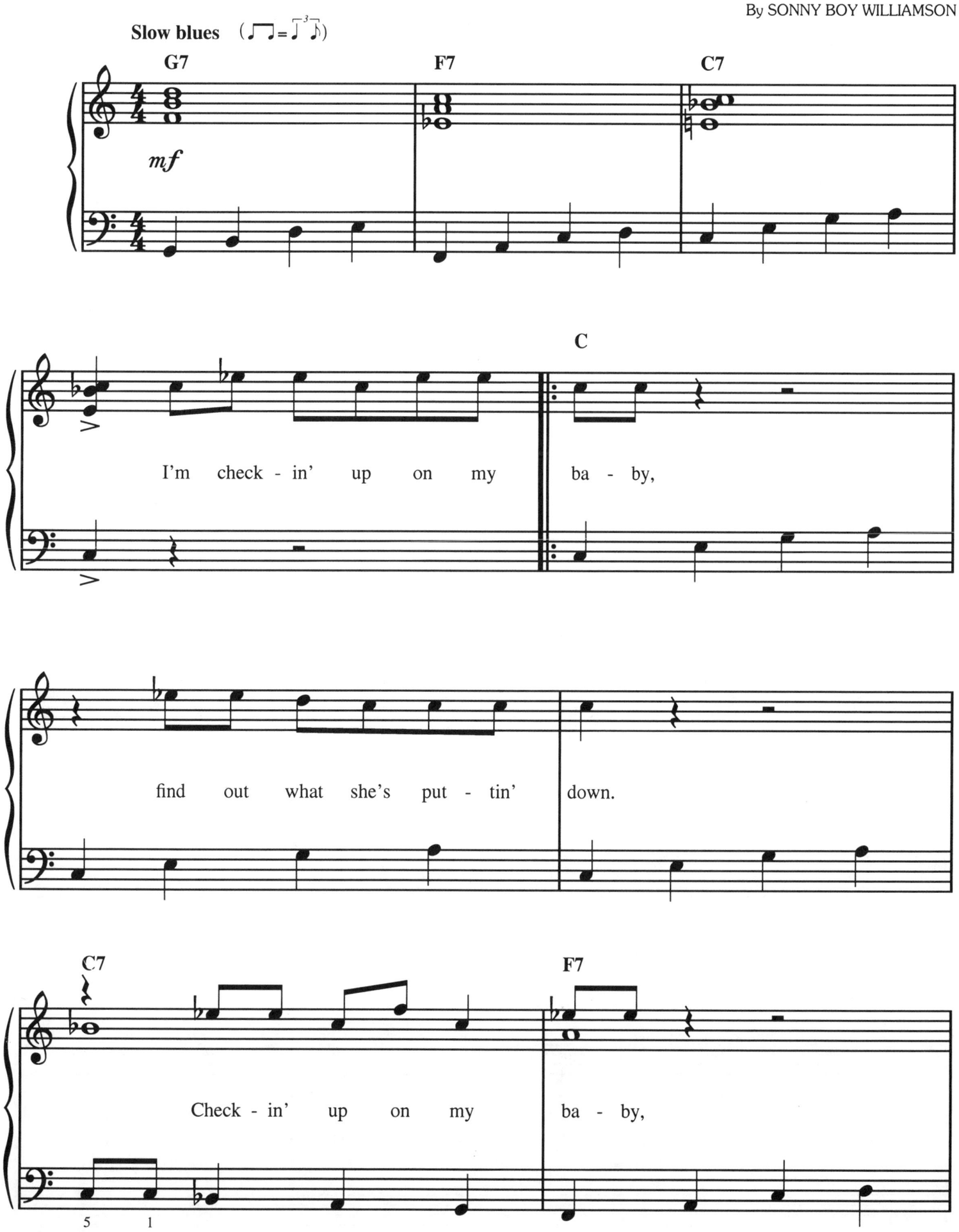

Copyright © 1965 (Renewed) by Arc Music Corp.
International Copyright Secured All Rights Reserved

C
find out what she's put - tin' down.
5
G7
So man - y nights and days.
F7
C
C7
I have been out of town.
I would-n't call
C
home,
and I would-n't e - ven write.

C7
F7
I would - n't call
home, ___
C
and I would-n't e - ven
write.
I caught me a
G7
F7
C
plane,
flew back _____ the same
night.
1.
2.
C7
C6/9
Check - in' up on my

CHICAGO BLUES

Words and Music by
LONNIE JOHNSON

© Copyright 1962 by MCA MUSIC PUBLISHING, A Division of MCA INC.
Copyright Renewed
International Copyright Secured All Rights Reserved
MCA music publishing

F7 C F7 C G7+
oth - er chump that's dropped in town.
My first night in Chi -
C7 F7 C C7
ca - go, my friends real-ly treat-ed me fine.
Then o - ver -
F7 C G7 C
night, they all changed like Day-light Sav-ing Time.
And ev-'ry-thing
G7 F7 C C7/E F F♯dim
I want-ed, I had to lay my mon-ey down on the line.

G7
C
F7
I said, "Ba - by, you're so love - ly. Your eyes shine like the stars a - bove.

C
C7
F7
You wear num-ber three shoes, yes, and wear num-ber five gloves."

C
G7
C7
G7
She said, "It's mon - ey I need.

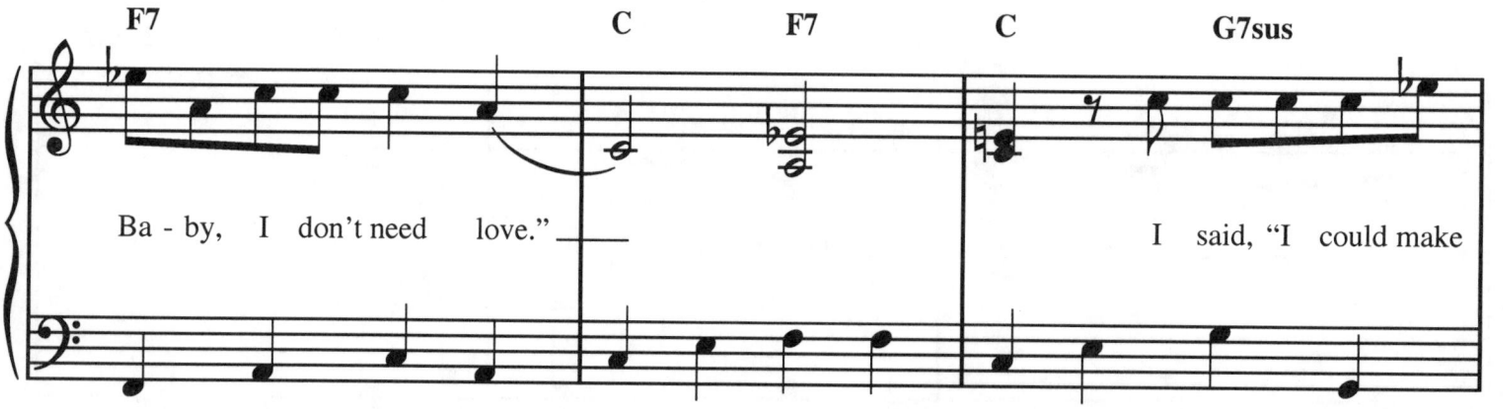
F7
C
F7
C
G7sus
Ba - by, I don't need love."
I said, "I could make

C
F7
C
you love me, dar - lin'.
Ba - by, I just bet I could.

C7
F7
You can learn to
love me, ba - by.
I knew you could."

C
G7
C
G7+
She says, "Lay your
mon - ey down,

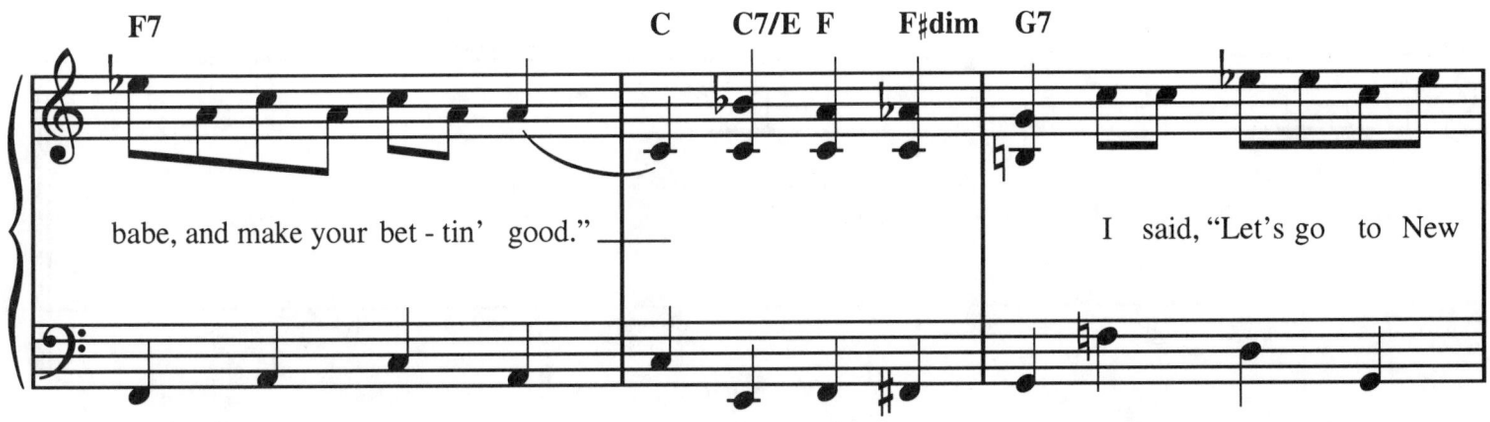
F7
C
C7/E
F
F♯dim
G7
babe, and make your bet - tin' good."
I said, "Let's go to New

F7
C
York, ba - by. I'll buy you an - y - thing you lack.
C7
F7
I will give you plen-ty mon-ey, gon-na buy you a nine-teen for-ty-two Cad - il - lac."
C
F7
C
G7+
She says, "I'm sor - ry. This fine round
F7
C
C7/E
F
F♯dim
C/G
G+
C
bod - y will be here when you get back."

CRAZY BLUES

Words and Music by
PERRY BRADFORD

© Copyright 1920 by MCA MUSIC PUBLISHING, A Division of MCA INC.
Copyright Renewed
International Copyright Secured All Rights Reserved
MCA music publishing

B♭
B♭m
F
(He She) makes me feel so blue.
I don't know what to do.
Some-times I sit and sigh

F7
C7
and then be - gin to cry 'cause
my best friend
said (his her) last
good -

F
C7
F7
bye.
There's a
change in the

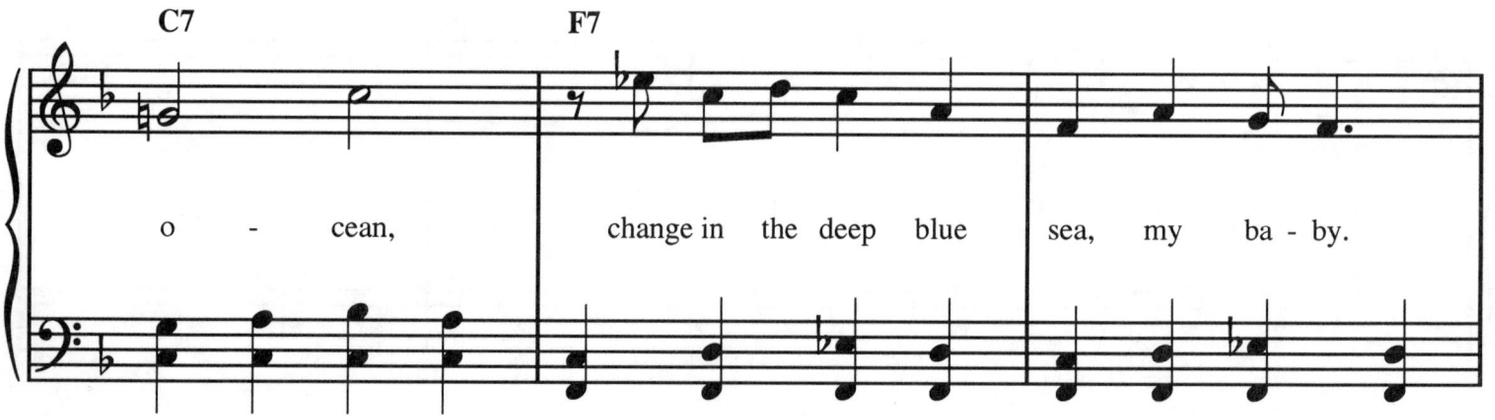
C7
F7
o - cean,
change in the deep blue
sea, my ba - by.

B♭7
C13
F
I'll tell you, folks, there
ain't no change in
me.
F♯dim7
Gm7
C7
Gm9
C7
My
love for that (man / gal)
will al - ways
F
B♭
B♭m6
F
D♭7 C7
F
be.
Now I can
read (his / her) let - ters.
I
F7
B♭7
sure can't read (his / her)
mind.
I thought (he's / she's) lov-in' me.

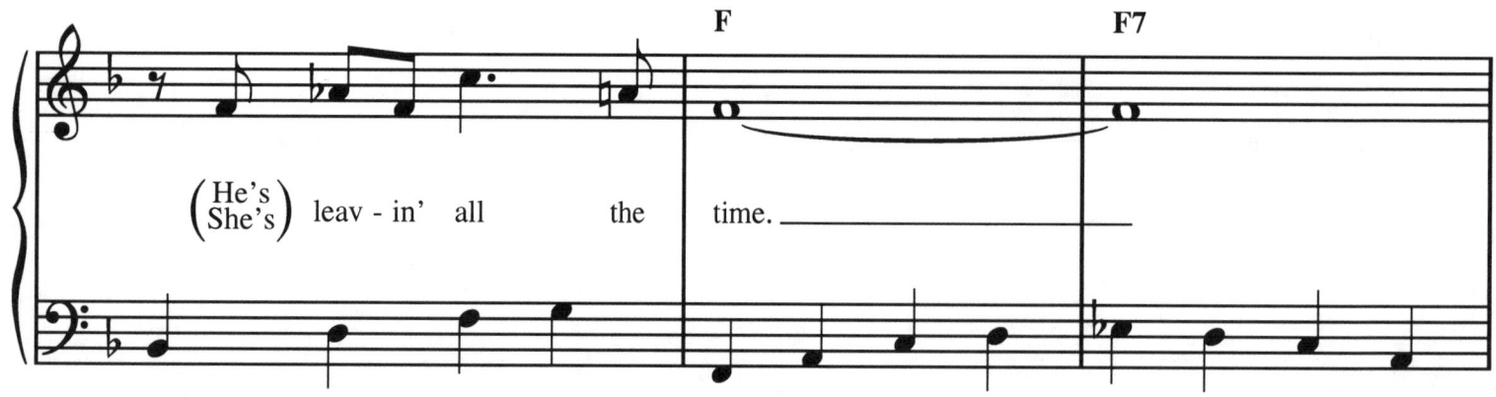
F
F7
(He's She's) leav - in' all the time.

C
B♭
F
Now I see my poor love was blind.

Gm7 Bdim C7
F
F7
Now I got the cra - zy blues

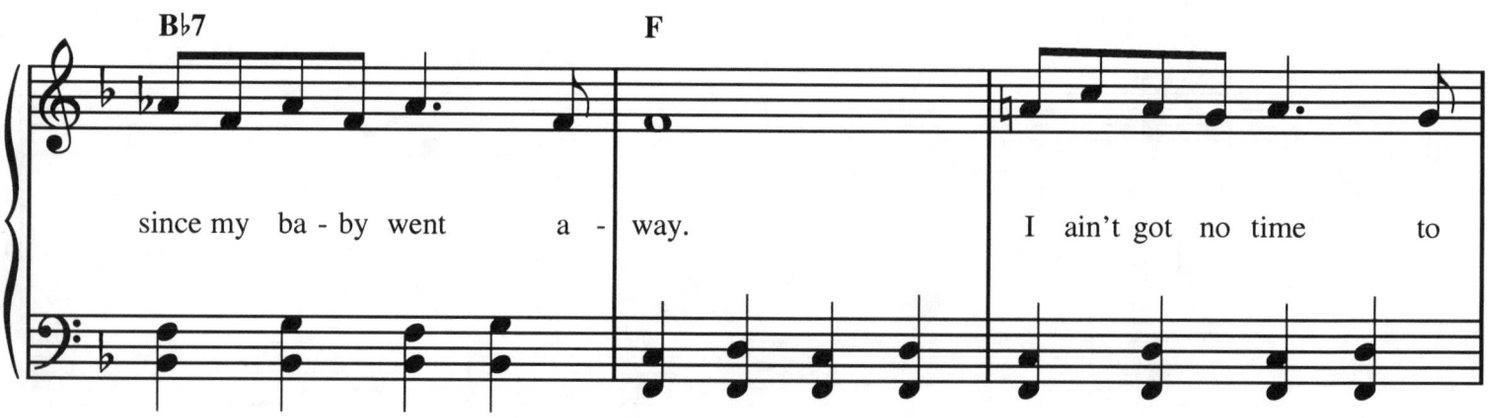
B♭7
F
since my ba - by went a - way.
I ain't got no time to

F7 G7 C7
lose. I must find (him her) to - day. Now the
F B♭7
doc-tor's gon-na do all that he can, but what you're gon-na need is an
F Dm Dm(maj7) Dm7 G7
un - der - tak - er man. I ain't had noth - in' but bad news.
C7 C7♯5 F F7/A B♭ D♭/B F/C C7♯5 F6/9
Now I got the cra - zy blues.

DOWN HEARTED BLUES

Words by ALBERTA HUNTER
Music by LOVIE AUSTIN

© Copyright 1922 by ALBERTA HUNTER and LOVIE AUSTIN
© Copyright 1949, 1963 by MCA MUSIC PUBLISHING, A Division of MCA INC.
Copyright Renewed
International Copyright Secured All Rights Reserved
MCA music publishing

B♭7
E♭7
blues.
me.
Once I was cra - zy
I've al - most wor - ried my -
A♭
'bout a (man. / gal.) (He / She) mis - treat - ed me all the
- self to death won - d'ring why (he / she) went a -
G7
F7
time. The next (man / gal) I get (he's / she's) got to
way. But just wait and see (he's / she's) gon - na
B♭7
C7
F7
B♭7
prom - ise me to be mine, all mine.
want me back some sweet day.

E♭
A♭
B♭7
1. Trou - ble, trou - ble, I've had it all my
2. world in a jug, the stop - per's in my
3.-6. (See additional lyrics)
E♭
E♭7
days.
hand.
Got the
3
1
A♭
B♭7
Trou - ble, trou - ble, I've had it all my
world in a jug, the stop - per's in my
E♭
E♭7
days.
hand.
It
Going to
3

Additional lyrics

3. Say, I ain't never loved but three (men / women) in my life.
   No, I ain't never loved but three (men / women) in my life,
   'Twas my (father, brother / mother, sister) and the (man / woman) who wrecked my life.

4. 'Cause (he / she) mistreated me and (he / she) drove me from (his / her) door,
   Yes, (he / she) mistreated me and (he / she) drove me from (his / her) door,
   But the Good Book says you'll reap just what you sow.

5. Oh, it may be a week and it may be a month or two,
   Yes, it may be a week and it may be a month or two,
   But the day you quit me honey, it's coming home to you.

6. Oh, I walked the floor and I wrung my hands and cried,
   Yes, I walked the floor and I wrung my hands and cried,
   Had the down hearted blues and couldn't be satisfied.

DIVING DUCK

Words and Music by
OTIS SPANN

© Copyright 1969 by DUCHESS MUSIC CORPORATION
DUCHESS MUSIC CORPORATION is an MCA company
Internaitonal Copyright Secured All Rights Reserved
MCA music publishing

F7
3
At the riv-er of

whis - key,
peo - ple, then
I was a div - ing duck.

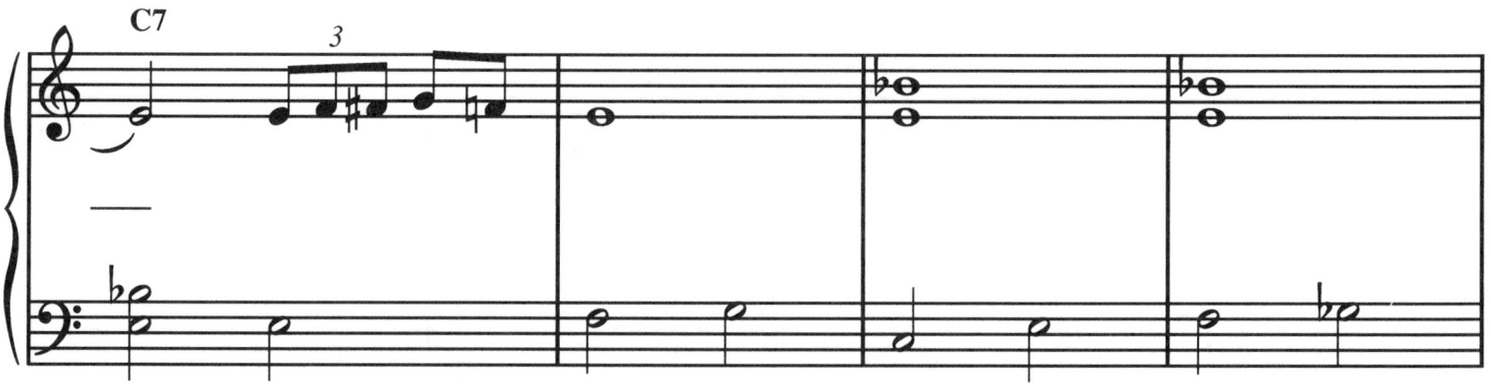
C7
3

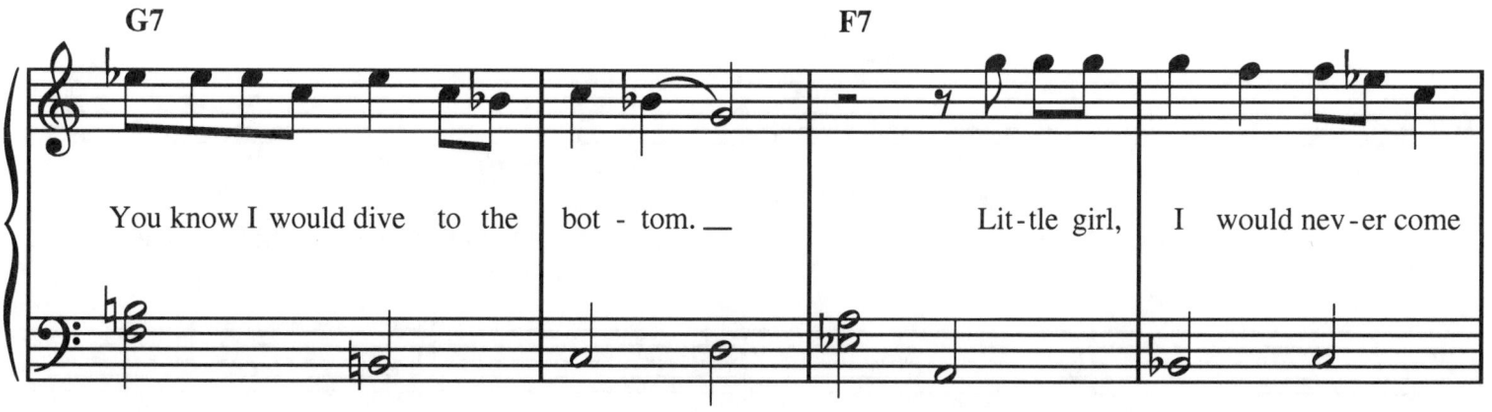
G7
F7
You know I would dive to the
bot - tom.
Lit-tle girl,
I would nev-er come

C7
G7
up.

C7
F7
One of these days, ba - by,
(Instrumental)
I'm gon-na leave you all a - lone.

C7

F7
Hey hey hey,
I got to leave you all a - lone.

C7
A♭7
G7
F7
You know I thought I had my - self a good thing,
but you broke
C7
G7
C7
up my hap - py home.
G7
C7
F7
I found out some - thing.
Blues is a

C7
both - er - a - tion on your mind.
F7
Oh, child, I found out some - thing.
C7
You know that blues is a both - er - a - tion on your mind.
G7
3
When I thought you were lov - ing

F7
me, wom - an, oh
you were leav - ing all the time.
C7
G7
C7
F7
Well now, this my sto - ry.
Lit - tle girl, it's all I have to say
C7
to you.

F7
Oh, you know this my ___ sto - ry. This is all I have to say _ to
C7
you.
G7
F7
You know I'm gon-na leave to - mor-row, _ ba-by, 'cause my love for you _ is
C C7/E F A♭/G♭ G7 B♭ C7
through.

EVERYDAY

(I Have The Blues)

By PETER CHATMAN

Copyright © 1952 (Renewed) by Arc Music Corporation and Fort Knox Music, Inc.
International Copyright Secured All Rights Reserved

D7
G
be-cause it's you I hate to
lose.
No-bod - y
C7
G
loves me,
no - bod - y seems to
care.
G7
C9
G6
No-bod - y
loves
me, no-bod - y seems to
care.
3
A7
D7
Speak-in' of
bad luck and trou - ble, well, you
know I've had my

G
G7
C7
share.
I'm gon-na
pack my suit - case,
mov-in' on down the
G
G7
C7
line.
Oh,
I'm
gon-na pack my
G
A7
suit-case,
move on down the
line.
Well, there ain't
no - bod - y
wor-ryin' and there
D7
G
ain't no - bod - y
cryin'.
Seems to me ev - 'ry

day, ev - 'ry day, ev - 'ry day I have the blues.
G7
C7
Ev - 'ry day, ev - 'ry day, ev - 'ry day, ev - 'ry day I have the
G
Am7
blues.
You see me wor - ry, ba - by, 'cause it's
Fine
D7
G
B♭dim
Am7 A♭maj7 G
you I ____ hate to lose.
No -

- bod - y loves me, no - bod - y seems to
G7
C7
care. No - bod - y loves me, no -
G
A7
3
- bod - y seems to care. Speak-in' of bad luck and trou - ble,
D7
G
D.S. al Fine
well, you know I've my share. Ev - 'ry

FINE AND MELLOW

Words and Music by
BILLIE HOLIDAY

Copyright © 1940 by Edward B. Marks Music Company
Copyright Renewed
International Copyright Secured All Rights Reserved
Used by Permission

C7/G
D♭7 C7
F
C7/G
low - est man
that I've ev - er
seen.
F
D♭9 C7 N.C.
Fm
B♭7
He wears
high draped pants,
stripes are real - ly yel -
F
Gm7
F/A
Gm7
F
F7
Fm
low.
He wears
high draped pants,
B♭7
F
C7/G
F/A
F♯dim
Gm7
C7
stripes are real-ly yel - low.
But when he
starts in to love me,

D♭7 C7 F F6 F F6 Fm
he's so fine and mel-low. Love will make you drink and gam-ble,

B♭7 F C7/G F7/A F7
make you stay out all night long, Love will

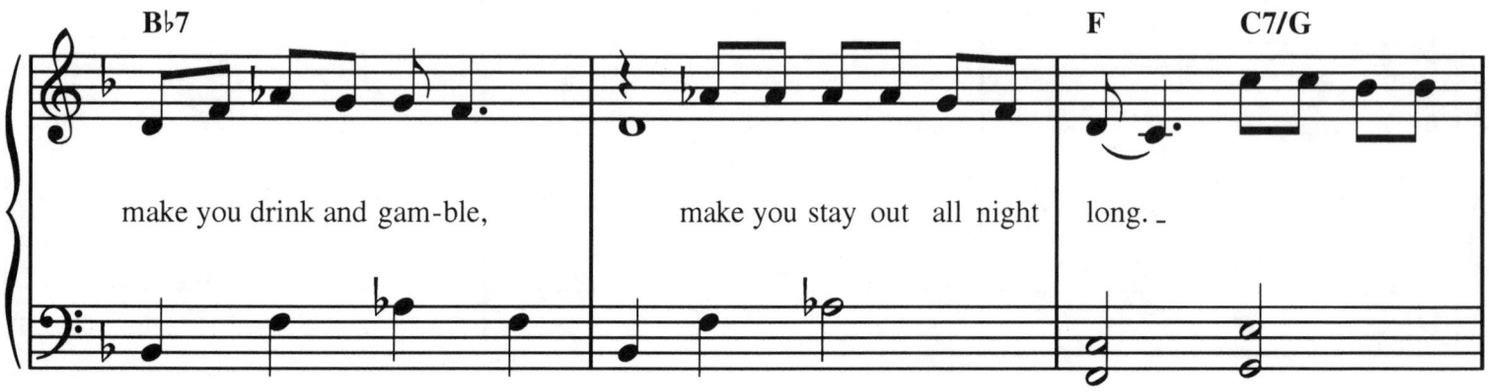
B♭7 F C7/G
make you drink and gam-ble, make you stay out all night long.

F/A C7♯5 D♭7 C7
Love will make you do things that you know is

F C7/G F/A D♭9 C7 N.C. F N.C.
wrong. But if you treat me right, ba - by,
F N.C. F C7/G F/A C7/G F F7 B♭7
I'll stay home ev-'ry day. If you treat me right, ba-by,
F C7/G F/A
I'll stay home ev - 'ry day. But you're so
C7 D♭7 C7 C7sus F C7/G
mean to me, ba - by, I know you're gon-na drive me a - way.

F D♭9 C7 N.C. Fm6 B♭7
Love is just like a fau - cet; it turns off and
F C7/G F/A F B♭7
on. Love is like a fau-cet; it turns off and
F C7/G F/A F♯dim7 Gm9 C7
on. Some-times when you think it's on, ba - by,
D♭7 C7 F E♭/G D♭9 C7♯9 F G♭9 F9
it has turned off and gone.

HEARTBREAK HOTEL

Words and Music by MAE BOREN AXTON,
TOMMY DURDEN and ELVIS PRESLEY

Copyright © 1956 Sony Tree Publishing Co., Inc.
Copyright Renewed
All Rights Administered by Sony Music Publishing, 8 Music Square West, Nashville, TN 37203
International Copyright Secured All Rights Reserved

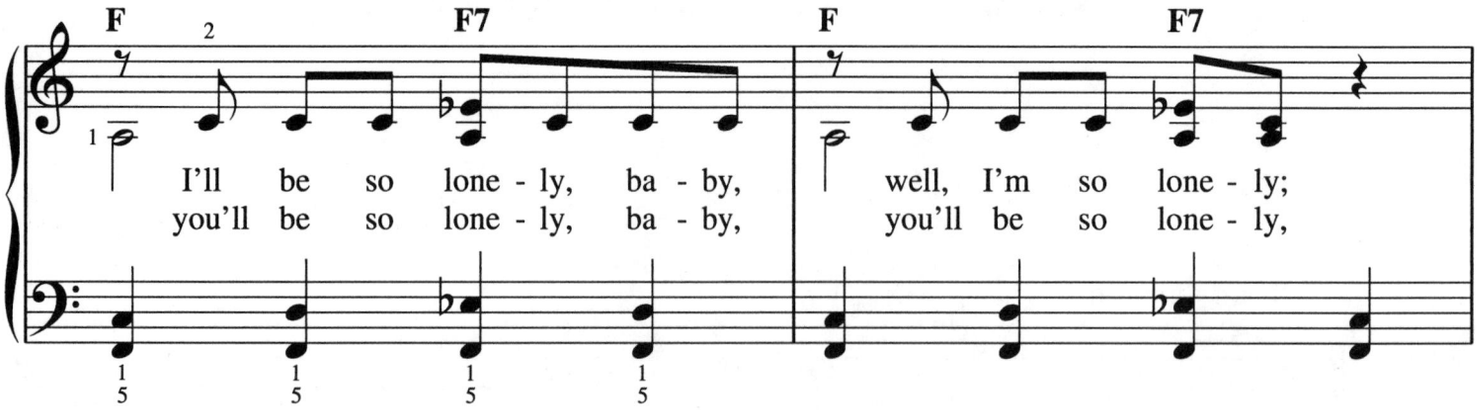
F
F7
F
F7
I'll be so lone - ly, ba - by, well, I'm so lone - ly;
you'll be so lone - ly, ba - by, you'll be so lone - ly,

G
C
I'll be so lone - ly ___ I could die. 2.,5. Al -
you'll be so lone - ly ___ you could die.

C
though it's al - ways crowd - ed you still can find some room for
bell - hop's tears are flow - in', the desk clerk's dressed in black. They

bro - ken heart - ed lov - ers to cry a - way their gloom.
been so long ___ on Lone - ly Street they ain't nev - er gon-na come back. ___ They get so

F
To Coda
They get so lone - ly, ba - by, they get so lone - ly.
they get so lone - ly, ba - by, they get so lone - ly.
G
They're so lone - ly they could
They're so lone - ly they could
1.
C
C/G
Opt. R.H. 8va ---
die.
3. Well, the
2.
C
C/G
D.S. al Coda
loco
die.
4. Well,
CODA
G
They're so lone - ly they could
C
C/G
C7
die.

A GOOD MAN IS HARD TO FIND

Words and Music by
EDDIE GREEN

Copyright © 1994 by HAL LEONARD CORPORATION
International Copyright Secured All Rights Reserved

D7 F7/E♭ A7/E D7/F♯ G
hap - pi - ness, it nev - er lasts a day; my
A7 A7/E♭ D7 G7
heart is al - most break - ing while I say: A good
A7 D7
man is hard to find; you al-ways get the oth - er
G7 Dm7 G7
kind. Just when you think that he is your pal, you

C N.C. C/G G7 C N.C.
look for him and find him fool - ing 'round some oth - er gal. Then you
A7 D7
rave, you e - ven crave to see him lay - ing in his
G9 C E♭dim
grave. So, if your man is nice, take
Dm7 A♭ Dm7 G7 C7 N.C.
my ad - vice, and hug him in the morn - ing,

C7 N.C.
kiss him ev - 'ry night,
C7 N.C.
give him plen - ty lov - in',
C A7 D7 Dm7 G7
treat him right, for a good man now - a - days is hard to
1.
C C♯dim7 Dm7 G7 N.C.
find.
A good
2.
C Dm7 Fm6/G C C6/9
find.

HELP ME

By SONNY BOY WILLIAMSON
and RALPH BASS

Copyright © 1963 (Renewed) by Arc Music Corp.
International Copyright Secured All Rights Reserved

I may have to wash, ___ may have to sew. I may have to
Am7
cook, I might mop the floor. But you help me, ba - by.
Em
I can't do it all by my - self. You know if you don't
B7
Am7
Em
help me, dar - ling, _ I'll find my - self some-bod - y else.

When I walk, you walk with me. And when I

Am
talk, you talk to me. Oh, babe,

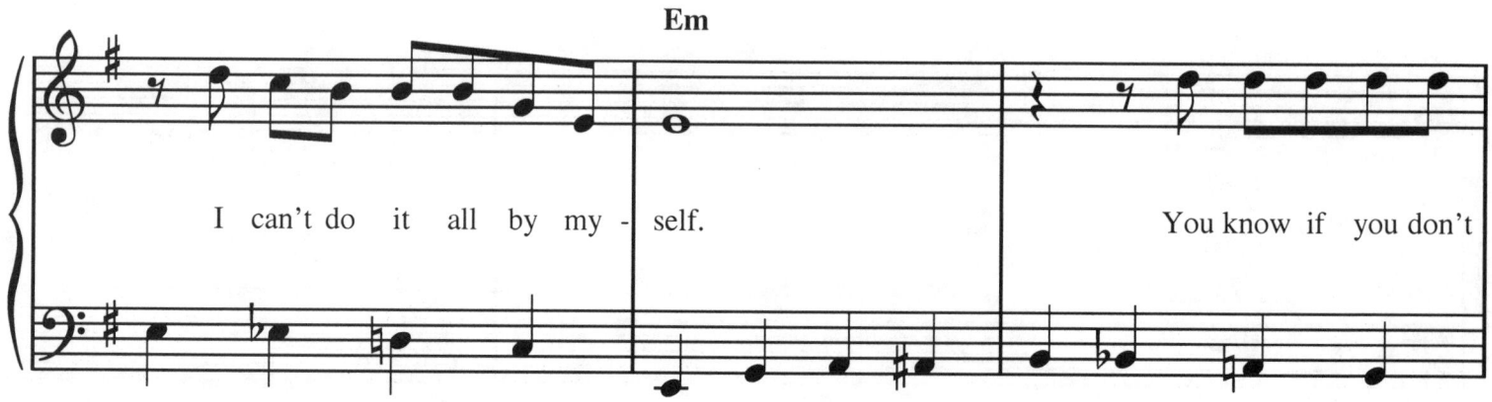
Em
I can't do it all by my - self. You know if you don't

B7
Am7
Em
help me, dar - ling, I'll have to find my - self some - bod - y else.

Bring my night - shirt.
Put on your morn-ing gown.
Am
Oh, bring me my night-shirt.
Put on your morn - ing
Em
B7
gown.
Do not know where she been,
Am7
Em
B7♯5
Em(maj7)
but I feel like ly - in'
down.

I'M A MAN

By ELLAS McDANIEL

Moderate rock tempo (♩♩ = ♩³♪)

Copyright © 1955 (Renewed) by Arc Music Corp.
International Copyright Secured All Rights Reserved

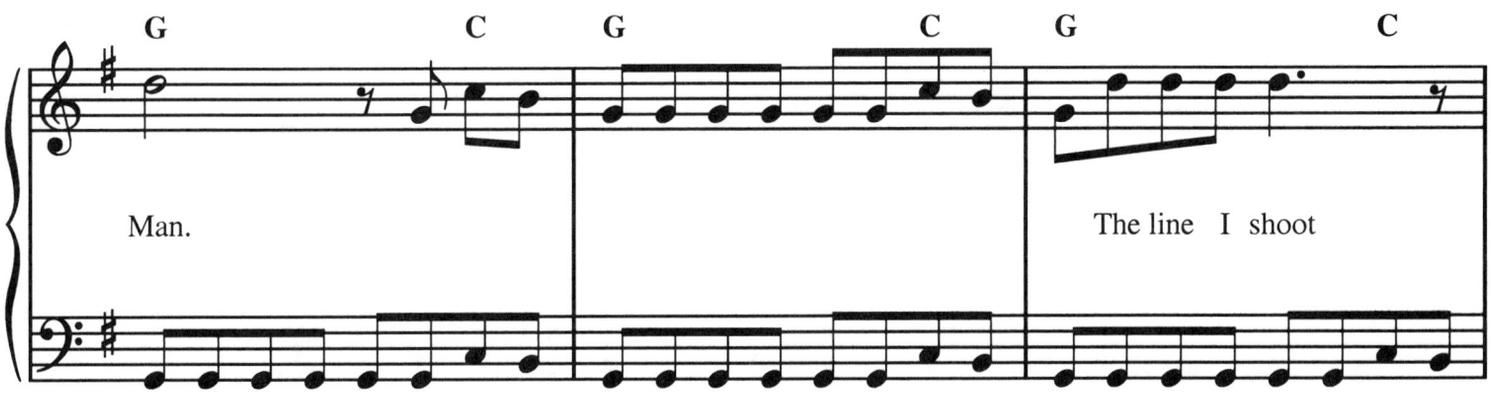
G C G C G C
Man.
The line I shoot

G C G C G C
will nev - er miss;
the way I make love to 'em,
they can't re - sist.

G C G C G C G C
Now I'm a man.
I spell M
A __
N, __

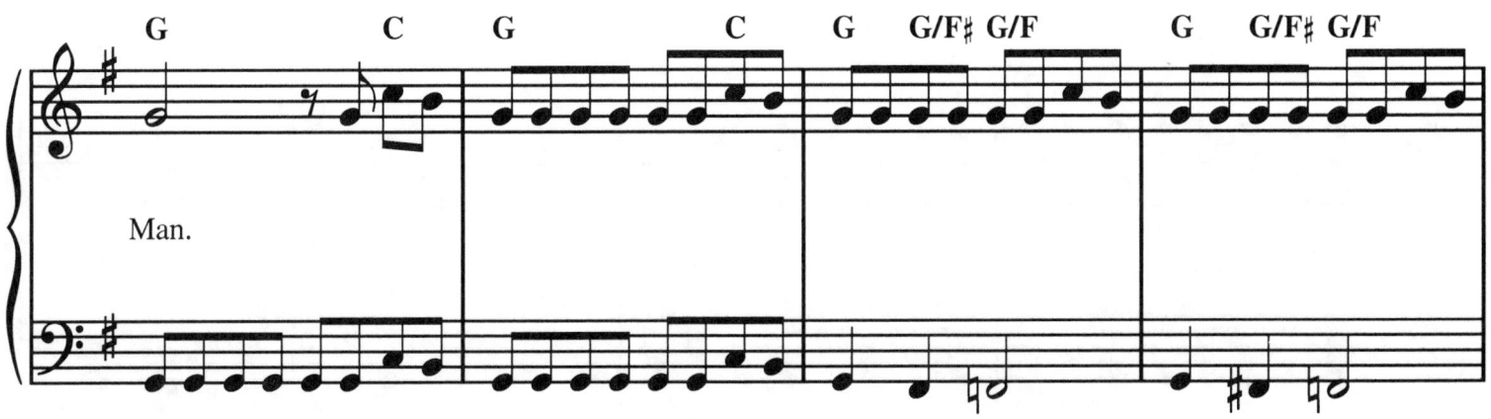
G C G C G G/F♯ G/F G G/F♯ G/F
Man.

G G/F G/D C/B G C G C G C
Go-in' back down
to Kan-sas to
G C G C G C G C
bring back a lit-tle girl
just like you.
Now I'm a man.
I spell M
G C G C G C G C
A __
N, __
Man.
G C G C G F F♯ G

IN THE EVENING

(When The Sun Goes Down)

Words and Music by
LEROY CARR

© Copyright 1935 by MCA MUSIC PUBLISHING, A Division of MCA INC.
Copyright Renewed
International Copyright Secured All Rights Reserved
MCA music publishing

G D7 G G♯dim Am7 D7sus
down. Oh, ain't it lone-some? Ain't it lone - some
west. Lord, ain't it hard to tell, hard to tell
E♭7 D7 G C7 G D7
when your lov - er can't be found when the sun goes down? Last
which one will treat you the best when the sun goes down? Good -
G C7
night I lay a - sleep - in', think - in' to my -
bye, sweet and lov - in' ba - by, you know I'm goin' a -
G G7 C7 C♯dim
self. Last night I lay a - sleep - in', think - in' to my -
way. Be back to see you some old rain - y

To Coda
G/D
D7
G
G♯dim
Am7
D7sus
self.
day.
Well, I thought he loved me,
E♭7
D7sus
G
C7
G
D7
D.S. al Coda
found he loved some-bod - y else when the sun went down. Well, the
CODA
G
G♯dim
Am7
D7sus
Well, in the eve - nin', in the eve - nin',
E♭7
D7
G
C7
G
when that ru - by sun goes down, when the sun goes down.

IT'S A LOW DOWN DIRTY SHAME

Words and Music by
OLLIE SHEPARD

© Copyright 1938, 1946 by MCA MUSIC PUBLISHING, A Division of MCA INC.
Copyright Renewed
International Copyright Secured All Rights Reserved
MCA music publishing

Gm7 C7 F7 B♭7
She's a no good wom-an, don't mean no one man no good.

F7 B♭7
She's a no good wom - an, don't

F7 F
mean no one man no good.
I don't

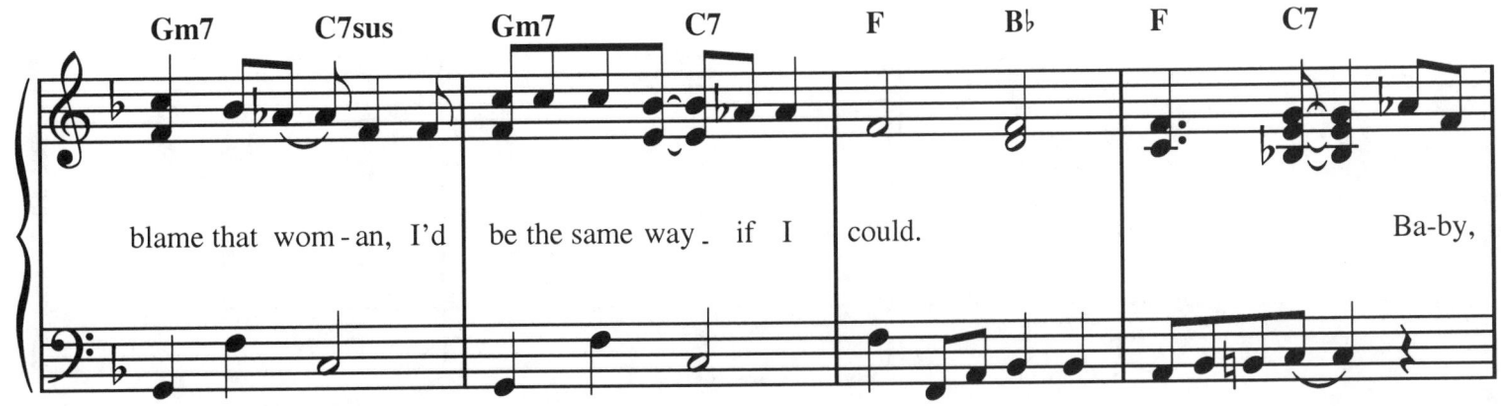
Gm7 C7sus Gm7 C7 F B♭ F C7
blame that wom - an, I'd be the same way if I could.
Ba-by,

G7 C7 G7 C7 F7
that's al - right, that's al - right for you. Ba - by,
B♭7 F7 D7
that's al - right, that's al-right for you. Ba - by,
G7 C7 G7 C7 1. F Ddim7
that's al - right, most an - y old thing you do.
Gm7 C7 2. F Ddim7 Gm7 C7 F
It's a do.

MAD ABOUT HIM, SAD WITHOUT HIM, HOW CAN I BE GLAD WITHOUT HIM BLUES

Words and Music by LARRY MARKES
and DICK CHARLES

© Copyright 1942 by MCA MUSIC PUBLISHING, A Division of MCA INC.
Copyright Renewed
International Copyright Secured All Rights Reserved
MCA music publishing

C7
G7
me.
Oh, the tears I've wast - ed would
F7
G7
C
sure - ly fill the deep blue sea.
I've got those
cry a - bout (him, her,) die with - out (him, her,)
Lor - dy, where am I with - out (him her)
C7
F7
blues.
He keeps me walk - in' on the floor,
She keeps me hang - in' 'round her door,

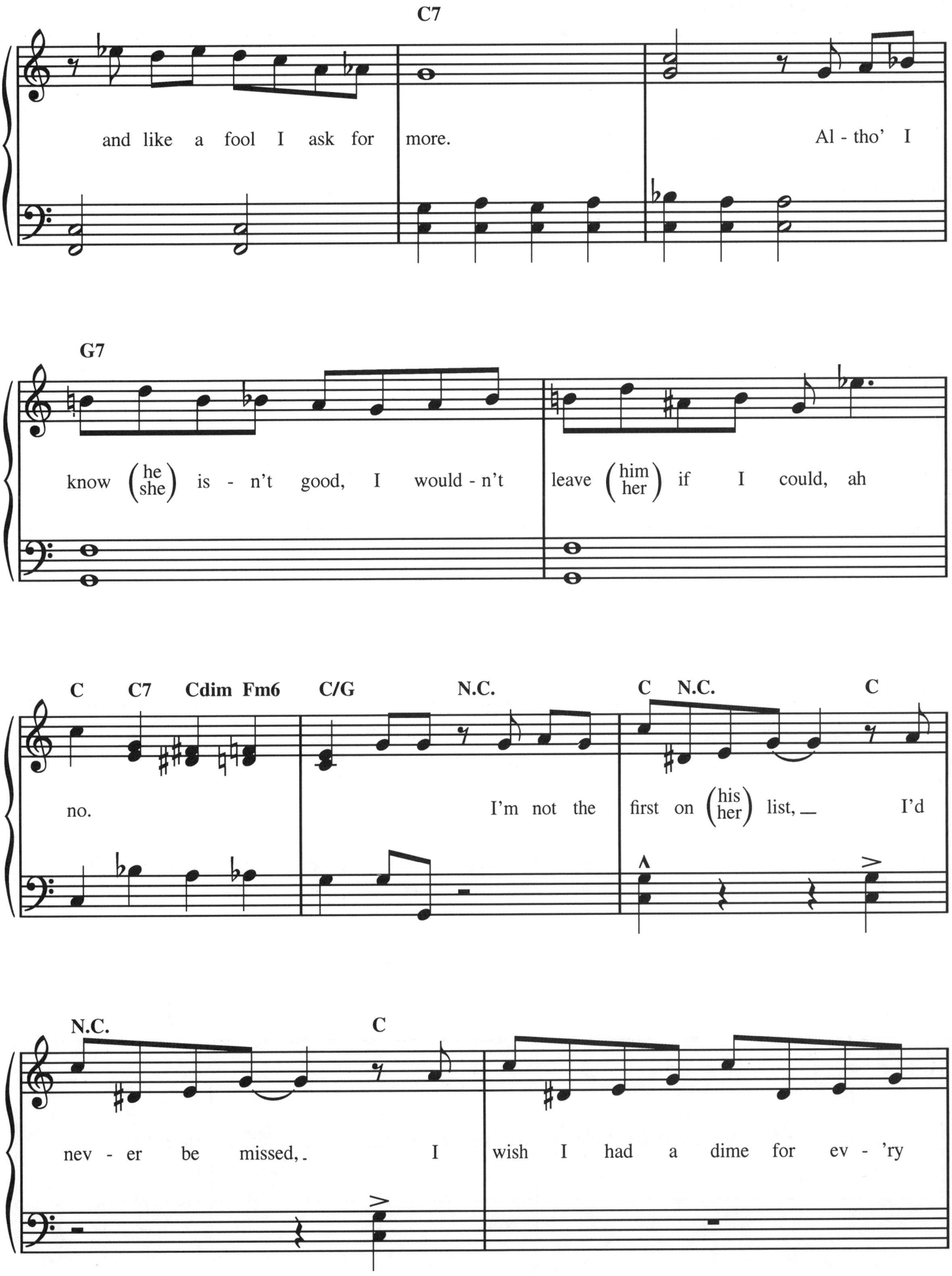
C7
and like a fool I ask for more.
Al - tho' I
G7
know (he she) is - n't good, I would - n't
leave (him her) if I could, ah
C C7 Cdim Fm6 C/G N.C. C N.C. C
no.
I'm not the
first on (his her) list,
I'd
N.C. C
nev - er be missed,
I
wish I had a dime for ev - 'ry

Gm Am Gm/B♭ C7 F
(gal he's / guy she's) kissed. I swear, I'd be a mil - lion -

C7 G7
aire. And yet I would-n't care as

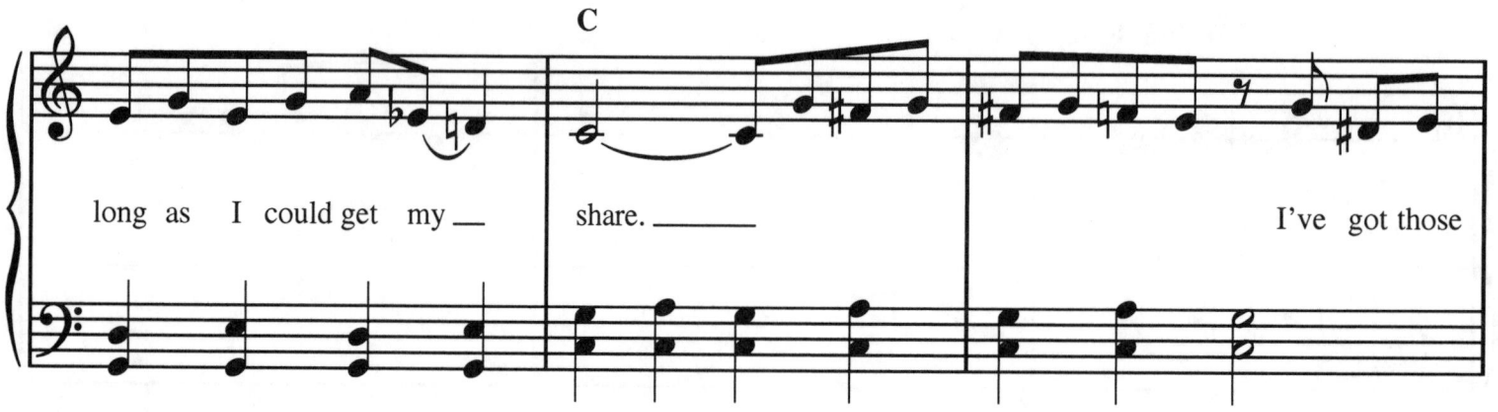
C
long as I could get my share. I've got those

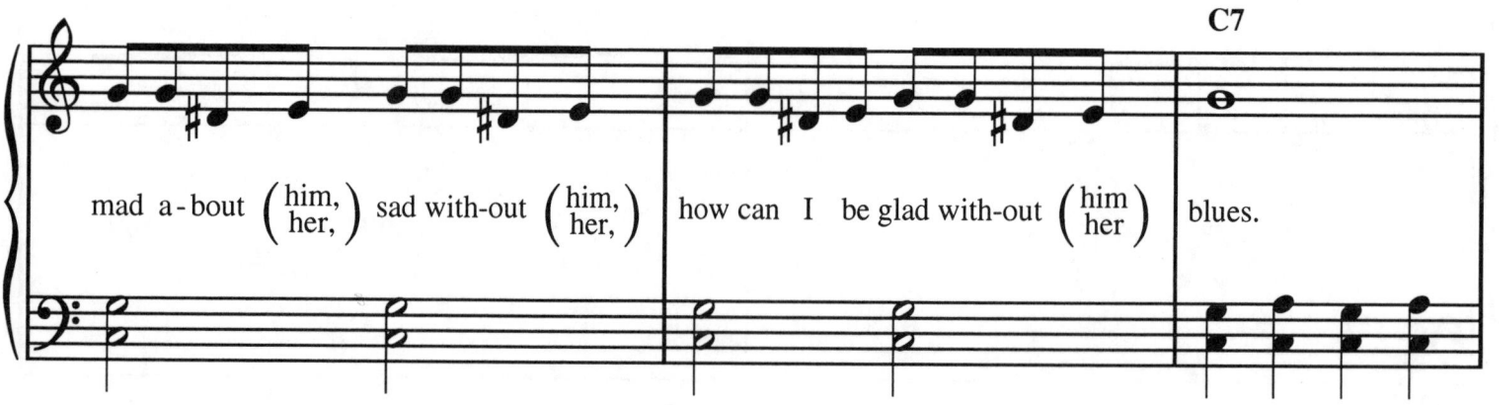
C7
mad a - bout (him, / her,) sad with-out (him, / her,) how can I be glad with-out (him / her) blues.

F7
(He She) makes my dreams go up in smoke, and then (he she) treats it like a
C7
joke.
He's just an orn - 'ry sort o' guy, and yet I'll
Al - tho' I know she is - n't true, there's not a
G7
love him till I die, poor me.
thing that I can do, poor me.
C
C7
Cdim
Fm6
1.
C/G
N.C.
I went to
2.
C/G
G9
C

MEAN OLD WORLD

By WALTER JACOBS

Copyright © 1970 by Arc Music Corporation
International Copyright Secured All Rights Reserved

G7
Try liv - ing by your - self.
D7
Can't get the one you're lov - in';
C7
G7
C
A7/C♯
have to use some - bod - y else.
G/D
E♭7 D7
G7
C7
I've got the blues;
gon - na pack my bags and

G7
go.
Yes,

C7
I've got the blues;
gon - na pack my bags and

G7
go.
Yes, I
D7
guess you real-ly don't love me,

C7
I'm just an un-luck-y so - and - so.
G G/B C A7/C♯ G/D A♭13 G13

MULE KICKING IN MY STALL

Words and Music by
McKINLEY MORGANFIELD

Copyright © 1970 Songs Of PolyGram International, Inc.
International Copyright Secured All Rights Reserved

F
kick-in' in my stall. I'm gon-na
she out of sight. But a
kick that mule a - way. He bet-ter
C7
B♭7
F7
kill that mule, had no trou-ble at all.
mule made me see the light.
kick in that mule 'cause he drove me a - way.
C7
F7
I got a mule been kick-in' in my
B♭7
stall. I've got a mule

F
been kick - in' in my
stall.
C7
If I
find that mule,
B♭7
it won't be no mule at
F7
all.
1.,2.
C7
The wom - an
I'm gon - na
3.
F
C7#9
F13

MEMPHIS BLUES

Words and Music by
W.C. HANDY

Copyright © 1994 by HAL LEONARD CORPORATION
International Copyright Secured All Rights Reserved

F
for - ty dol - lars down. If you don't

C7
be my (man, ___ / gal, ___) your ba - by's gon - na shake this

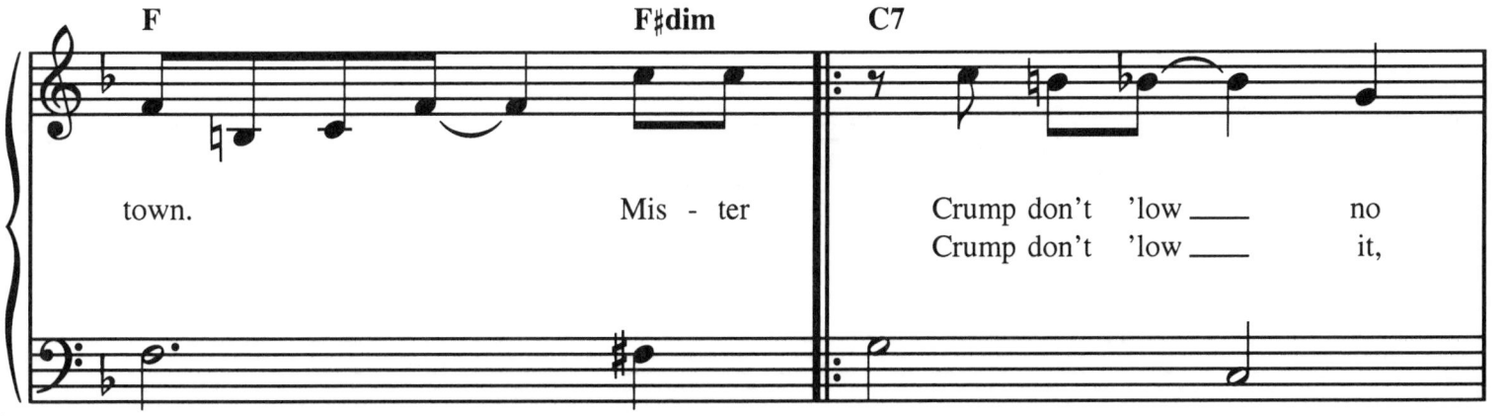
F
F♯dim
C7
town. Mis - ter
Crump don't 'low ___ no
Crump don't 'low ___ it,

F
eas - y rid - ers here.
ain't goin' have _ it here.

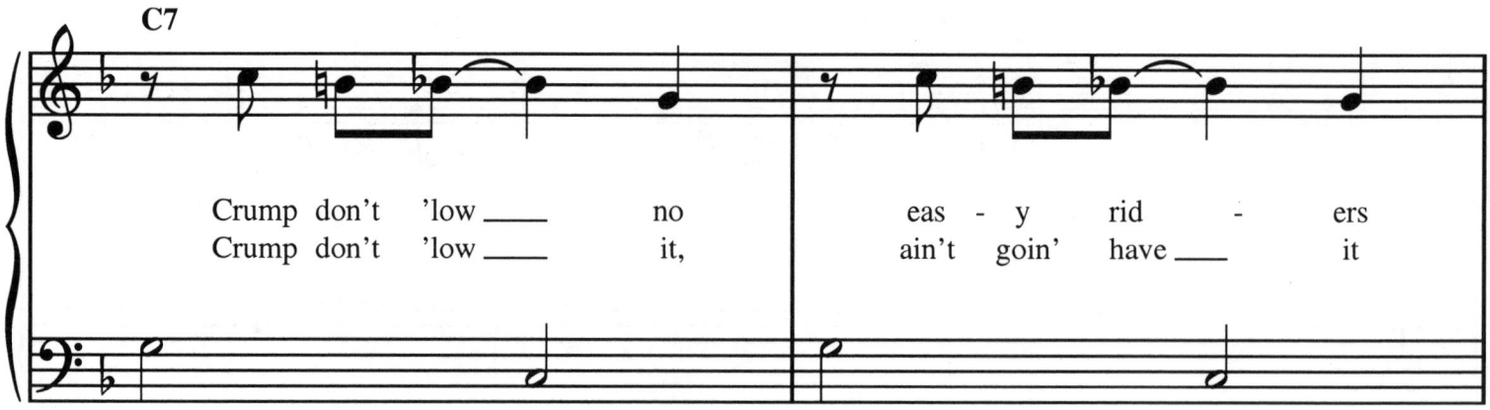
C7
Crump don't 'low ___ no
Crump don't 'low ___ it,
eas - y rid - ers
ain't goin' have ___ it

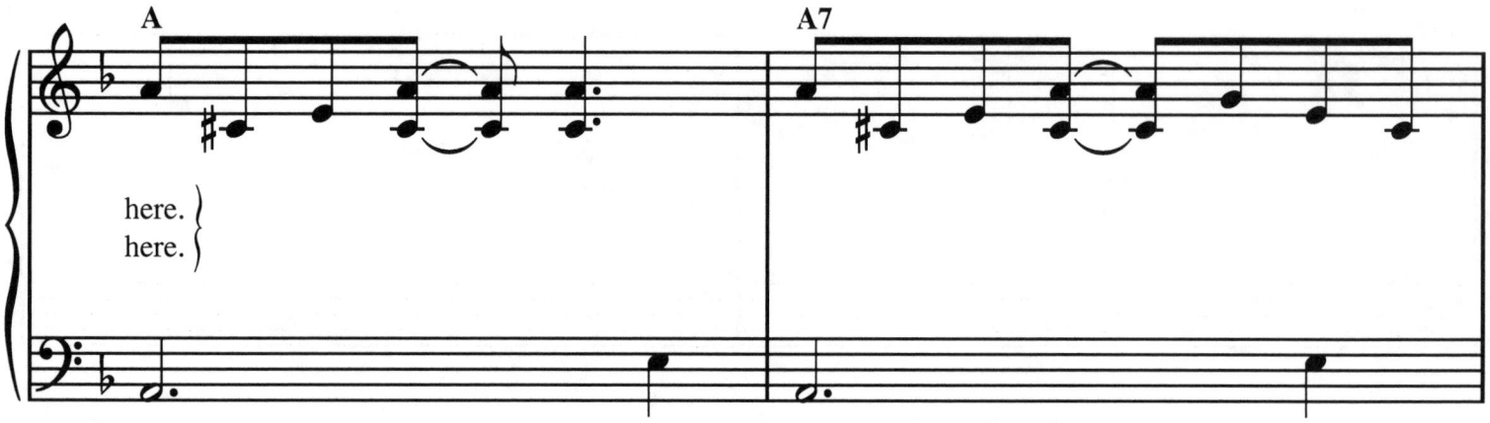
A
A7
here.
here.

D7
G7
We don't care __ what Mis - ter
Crump don't 'low, __
we gon - na bar'l - house

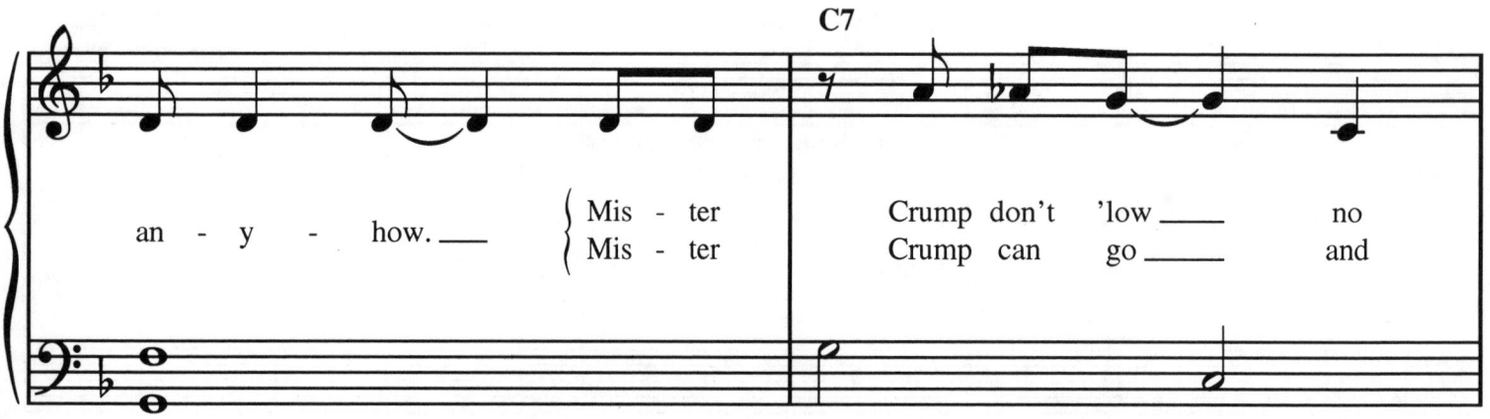
C7
an - y - how. ___
Mis - ter
Mis - ter
Crump don't 'low ___ no
Crump can go ___ and

1.
F
N.C.
F♯dim
eas - y rid - ers here.
catch his - self some
2.
F
C7
air.
F
N.C.
I'm go - in'
B♭
down the riv - er, go - in' down to the riv - er, goin' to

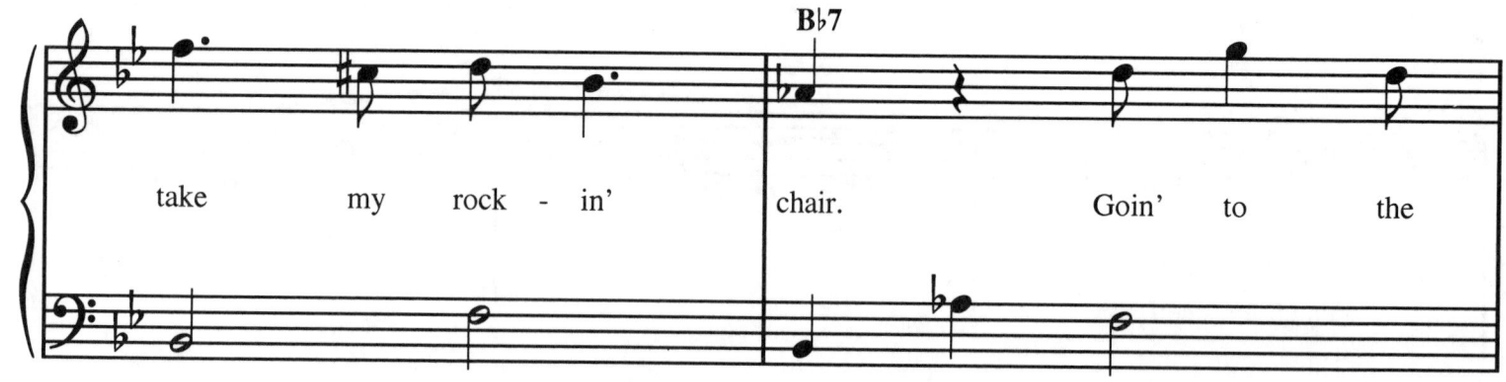
B♭7
take my rock - in' chair. Goin' to the

E♭
B♭
N.C.
riv - er, ___ goin' to take my rock - in' chair.

F7
Blues over - take me, goin' to rock a - way from

B♭
N.C.
B♭
here. Oh, the Mis - sis - sip - pi Riv - er,

B♭7
Mis - sis - sip - pi Riv - er so deep an' wide, I said the
E♭
B♭ N.C.
Mis - sis - sip - pi Riv - er's so deep an' wide.
F7
(Man Gal) I love, (he she) is on the oth - er
B♭ B♭7 B♭dim E♭m6 B♭
side.

MILK COW BLUES

Words and Music by
KOKOMO ARNOLD

© Copyright 1934 by MCA MUSIC PUBLISHING, A Division of MCA INC.
Copyright Renewed
International Copyright Secured All Rights Reserved
MCA music publishing

G6
D7
do?"
Now you look
might-y well this morn-in', but I
C9
G
G6 G♯dim7 D7
can't get a - long with
you.
How can
G6
C9
G
I do right, ba - by,
when you won't do right your -
self?
G7
C9
How can
I do right, ba - by,
when you won't do right your -

G6
D7
self?
If
my good gal quits me,
C9
G6
G♯dim7 D7
don't want no - bod - y
else.
Now that
G
C7
G
big bell is ring - in',
lit - tle bell is bare-ly at
all.
G7
C7
Big
bell is ring - in',
lit - tle bell is bare-ly at

G6
D7
all.
I'm low and dis - gust - ed,

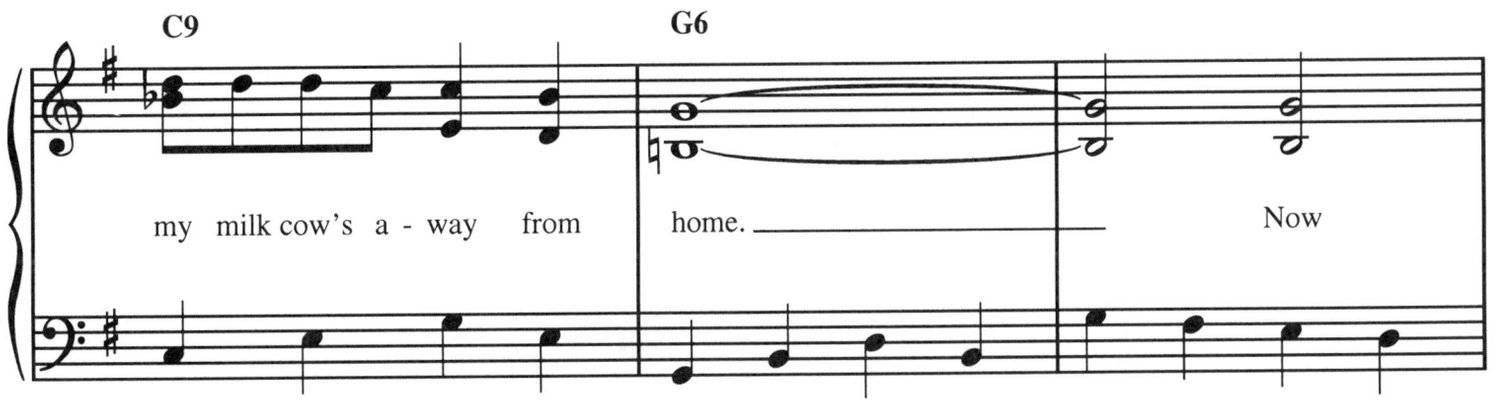
C9
G6
my milk cow's a - way from home.
Now

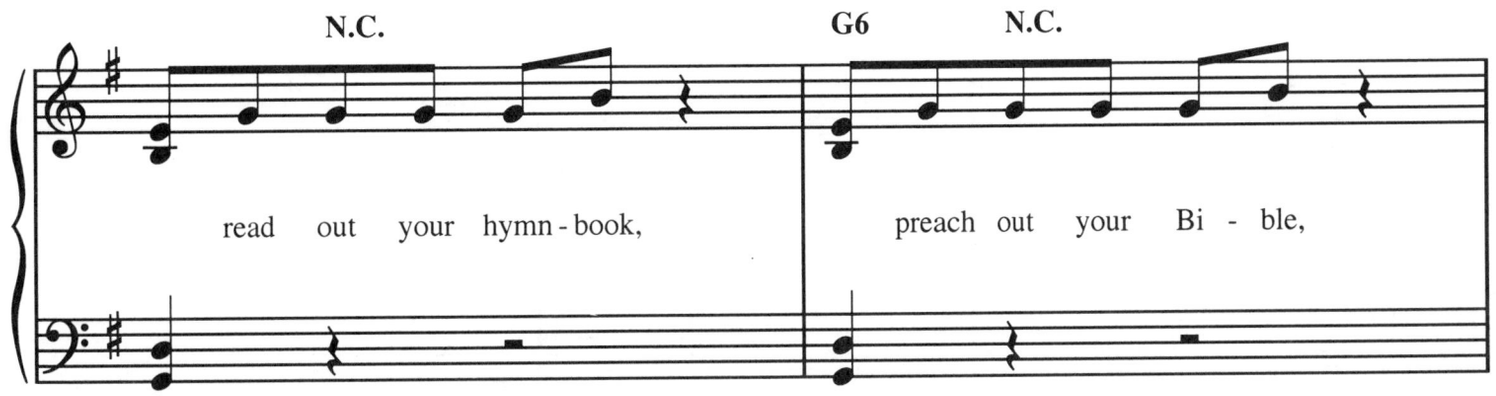
N.C.
G6
N.C.
read out your hymn - book,
preach out your Bi - ble,

G6
N.C.
G7
1
fall on your knees and pray to God to help you.
You're gon - na

C7
G6
need, you're gon - na need my help some - day.
D7
C9
I said, "Ma - ma, quit your sin - nin',
please quit your low - down
G G7 Gdim Cm6 G
G6 N.C.
ways."
Now I woke up this mor - nin',
G6 N.C.
G6 N.C.
3
looked out - doors,
my milk cow's gone, I know by the

Additional Verses

2. My blues fell this mornin' and my love came falling down,
   My blues fell this mornin' and my love came falling down,
   I may be a low-down dog, mama, but please don't dog me around.

3. It takes a rockin' chair to rock, a rubber ball to roll,
   Takes a long, tall, sweet gal to satisfy my soul,
   Lord, I don't feel welcome, no place I go,
   'Cause the woman I love done throwed me from her door.

MY BABY LEFT ME

Words and Music by
ARTHUR CRUDUP

Copyright © 1956 by Elvis Presley Music, Inc.
Copyright Renewed and Assigned to Elvis Presley Music (Administered by R&H Music)
International Copyright Secured All Rights Reserved

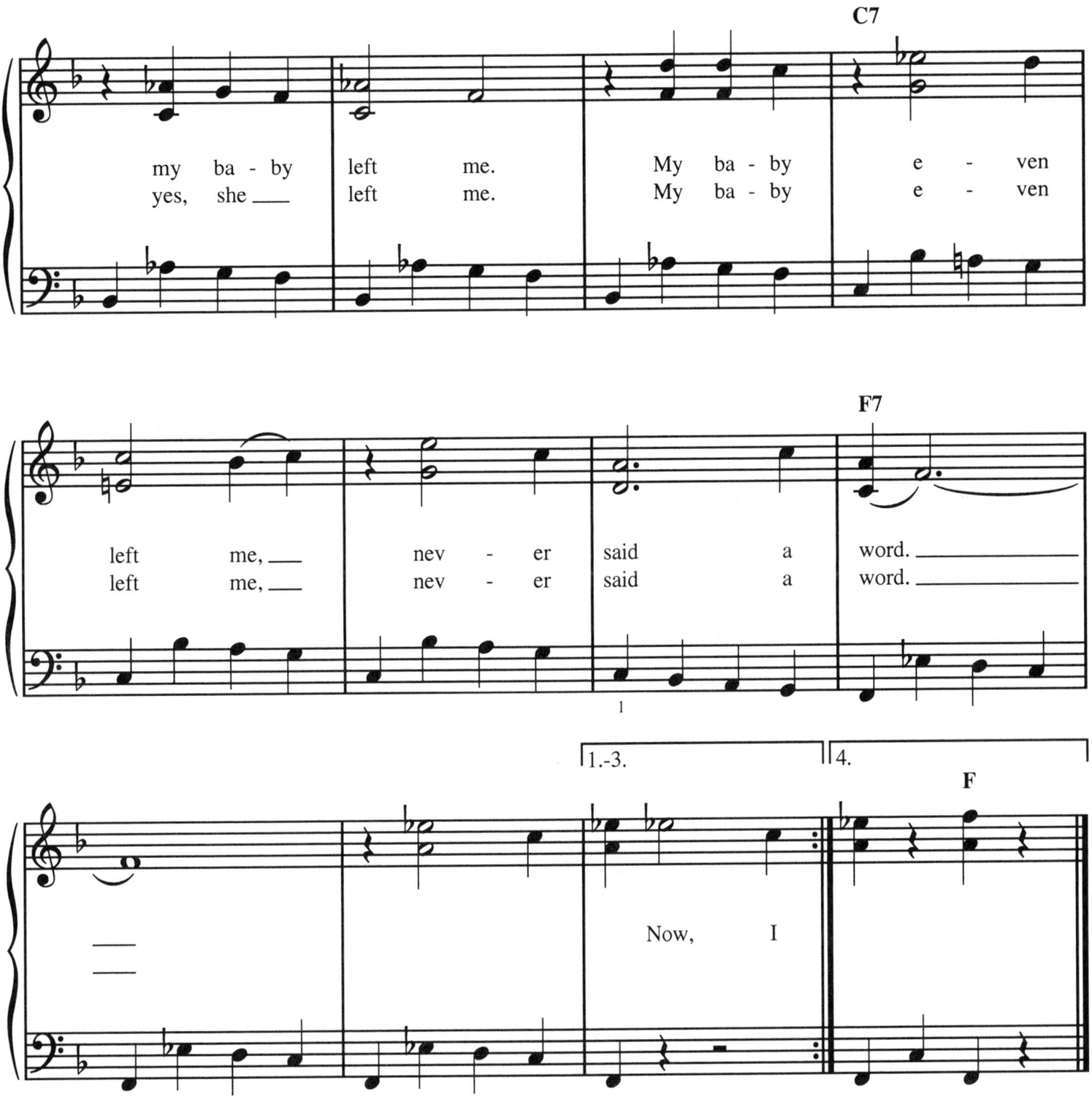

Additional Lyrics

3. Baby, one of these mornings, Lord, it won't be long.
   You'll look for me and, baby, and Daddy, he'll be gone.
   You know you left me, you know you left me.
   My baby even left me, never said goodbye.

4. Now, I stand at my window, wring my hands and moan.
   All I know is that the one I love is gone.
   My baby left me, you know she left me.
   My baby left me, never said a word.

PINETOP'S BLUES

Words and Music by
PINETOP SMITH

© Copyright 1929, 1941 by MCA MUSIC PUBLISHING, A Division of MCA INC.
Copyright Renewed
International Copyright Secured All Rights Reserved
MCA music publishing

F7
C7
She thinks she can love ev - 'ry - bod - y
I'm gon - na bur - y that wom - an
B♭7
F
F7
Fdim
B♭m6
and mis - treat poor me.
if she don't leave me a - lone.
F
F♯dim
C7
F
Now I cooked her break - fast, e - ven
I can't use no wom - an if she
B♭7
F
car - ried it to her bed.
can't help me lose the blues.

F7
B♭7
Now I cooked her break - fast, e - ven
I can't use no wom - an if she
car - ried it to her bed.
can't help me lose the blues.
F
F7
4
Now she
Go - in'
C7
B♭7
took one bite and threw the tea - cup at poor Pine - top's
down on State Street just to buy me a gal - lon of
1.
2.
F F7 Fdim B♭m F F♯dim C7
F C7♯5 F9
head.
booze.
I'm gon - na

ST. LOUIS BLUES

Words and Music by
W.C. HANDY

Copyright © 1990 by HAL LEONARD CORPORATION
International Copyright Secured All Rights Reserved

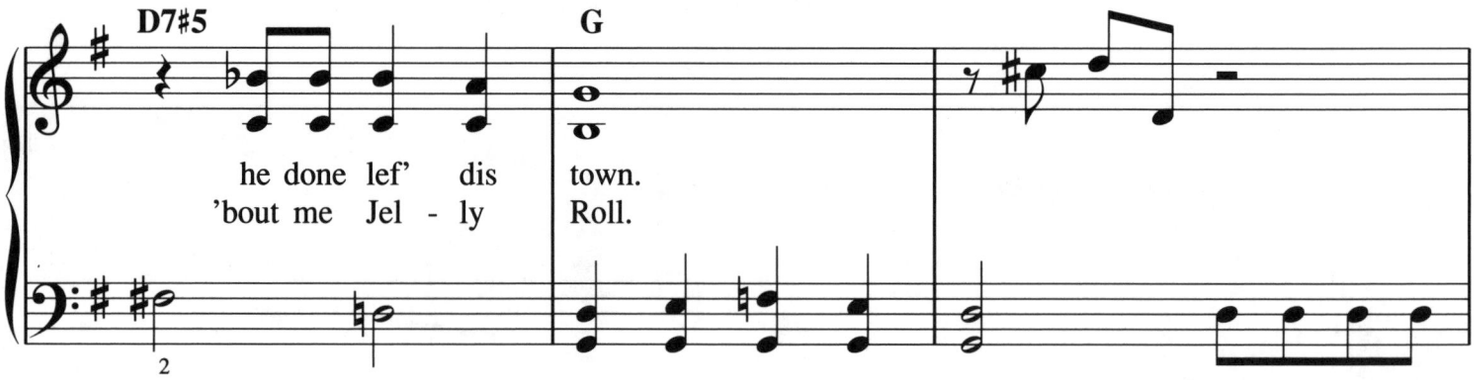
D7#5
G
he done lef' dis town.
'bout me Jel - ly Roll.

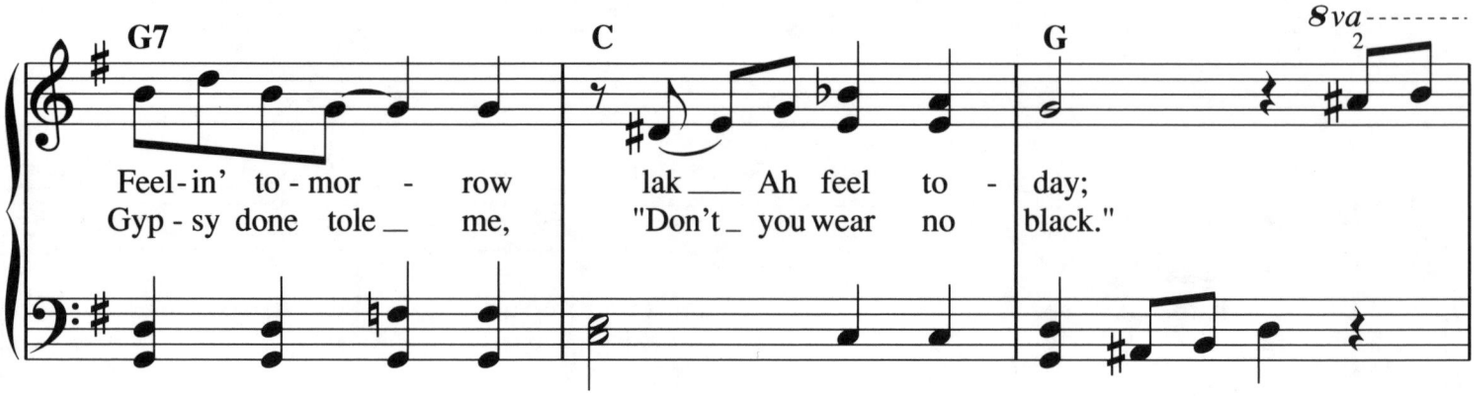
G7
C
G
8va
Feel-in' to-mor - row lak___ Ah feel to - day;
Gyp - sy done tole_ me, "Don't_ you wear no black."

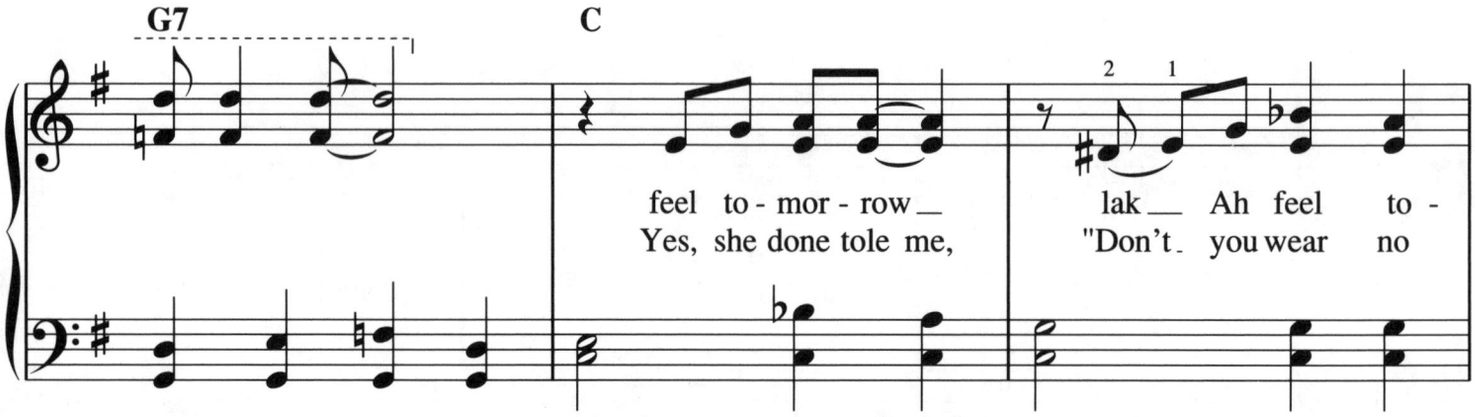
G7
C
feel to - mor - row_ lak___ Ah feel to -
Yes, she done tole me, "Don't_ you wear no

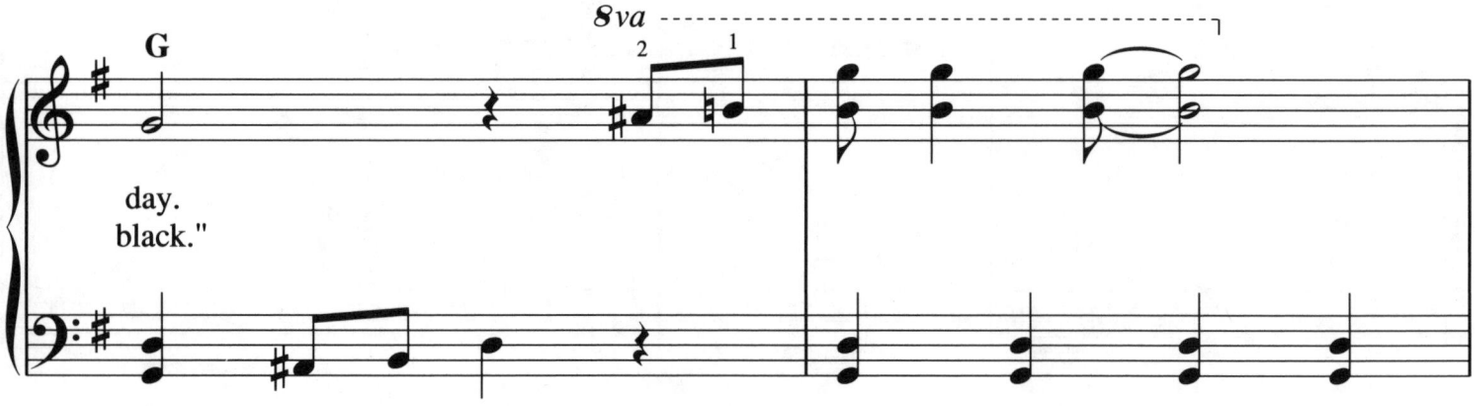
G
8va
day.
black."

D7
D7#5
G
I'll pack my trunk _ make me get a - way.
Go to St. Lou - is you can win him back.
Gm
St. Lou - is wom - an _____
Help me to Cai - ro, _____
Cm
Cdim7
D7
wid her dia - mon' rings pulls dat
make St. Louis by ma - self; git to
man 'roun' _ by her a - pron strings.
Cai - ro, ___ find my ole friend Jeff.
Gm

Cm7
Cdim7
'Twaint for pow - der _ an' for store_ bought
Gwine to pin ma - self close to ___ his
D7
hair de man I love _
side. If Ah flag his train _
Gm
A7/E
D7
would not gone no - where. _ Got me
I sho' can ride. _ I ___
G G6 G G6 G G6 G G6 G
St. Lou - is Blues jes as blue as ___ Ah ___ can be.
love dat ___ man lak a school boy _ loves ___ his pie;

C
Dat man got a heart lak a rock cast in the
lak a Ken - tuck - y Col' - nel loves his mint an'
G
sea. or else he would - n't have
rye. I'll love ma ba - by
G/D
D7
gone so far from
til the day Ah
1.,2.
G
me.
die.
(Spoken:) Dog-gone it!
3.
G
Jack.
rit.
G7

ROCK ME BABY

Words and Music by JOE JOSEA
and B.B. KING

Copyright © 1964 by Powerforce Music and Sounds of Lucille
Copyright Renewed
All Rights Administered by Careers-BMG Music Publishing, Inc.
International Copyright Secured All Rights Reserved

F7
Rock me ba - by,
Want you to roll me, ba - by,
Hey, rock me, pret - ty ba - by,
C7
hon - ey rock me all night long.
like you roll a wa - gon wheel.
ba - by, rock me slow.
G7
I want you to rock me, ba - by,
Want you to roll me, ba - by,
Will you rock me, ba - by,
F7
like my back ain't got no
you don't konw how it makes me
'til I want no
C7
bone.
feel.
more?
1.,2.
G7 A♭7 G7
3.
C G7♯5 C9

SAINT JAMES INFIRMARY

Words and Music by
JOE PRIMROSE

Copyright © 1994 by HAL LEONARD CORPORATION
International Copyright Secured All Rights Reserved

Additional lyrics

2. Went up to see the doctor.
"She's very low," he said.
Went back to see my baby;
Great God! She was lyin' there dead.

3. I went down to old Joe's bar-room
On the corner by the square.
They were servin' the drinks as usual,
And the usual crowd was there.

4. On my left stood Joe McKennedy,
His eyes blood-shot red.
He turned to the crowd around him,
These are the words he said:

5. Let her go, God bless her,
Wherever she may be.
She may search this wide world over,
She'll never find a man like me.

6. Oh, when I die please bury me
In my high-top Stetson hat.
Put a gold piece on my watch chain
So they'll know I died standin' pat.

7. Get six gamblers to carry my coffin,
Six chorus girls to sing my song.
Put a jazz band on my tail-gate
To raise hell as we go along.

8. Now that's the end of my story;
Let's have another round of booze.
And if anyone should ask you, just tell them
I've got the St. James Infirmary Blues.

SMOKESTACK LIGHTNING

By CHESTER BURNETT

Copyright © 1956 (Renewed) by Arc Music Corporation
International Copyright Secured All Rights Reserved

Additional Lyrics

3. Well, tell me, baby,
   Where did you stay last night?
   Well, don't you hear me crying?
   Boo-hoo, boo-hoo, boo-hoo.

4. Well, stop your train,
   Let us go for a ride.
   Well, don't you hear me crying?
   Boo-hoo, boo-hoo, boo-hoo.

5. Well, fare thee well,
   Never see you no more.
   Well, don't you hear me crying?
   Boo-hoo, boo-hoo, boo-hoo.

SUGAR BLUES

Words by LUCY FLETCHER
Music by CLARENCE WILLIAMS

© Copyright 1919 by MCA MUSIC PUBLISHING, A Division of MCA INC. and GREAT STANDARDS MUSIC PUBLISHING COMPANY
Copyright Renewed
All Rights for GREAT STANDARDS MUSIC PUBLISHING COMPANY Administered by THE SONGWRITERS GUILD OF AMERICA
International Copyright Secured All Rights Reserved
MCA music publishing

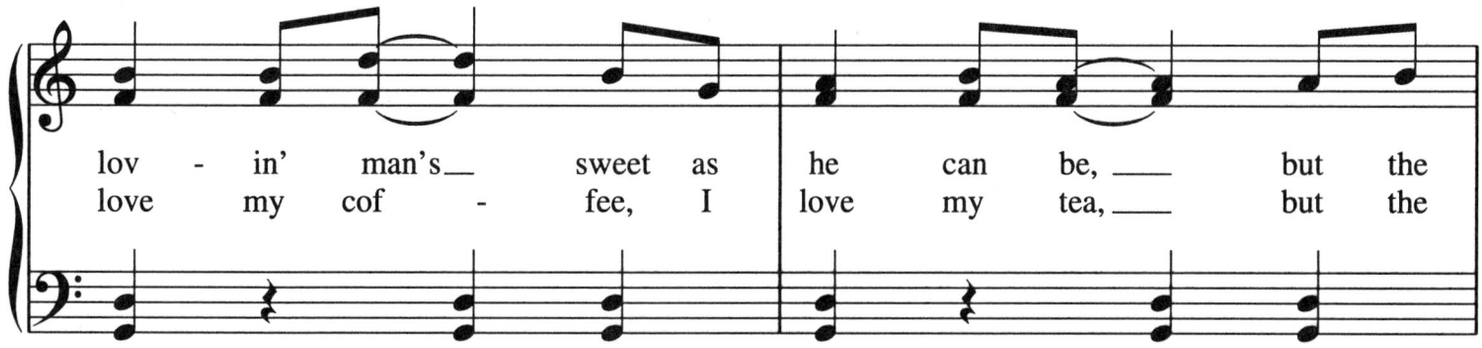
lov - in' man's sweet as he can be, but the
love my cof - fee, I love my tea, but the

C7
dog - gone fool turned so - ur on me.
dog - gone cream turned so - ur on me.

I'm so un - hap - py, I feel so bad, I could

F A7 Dm
lay me down and die. You can

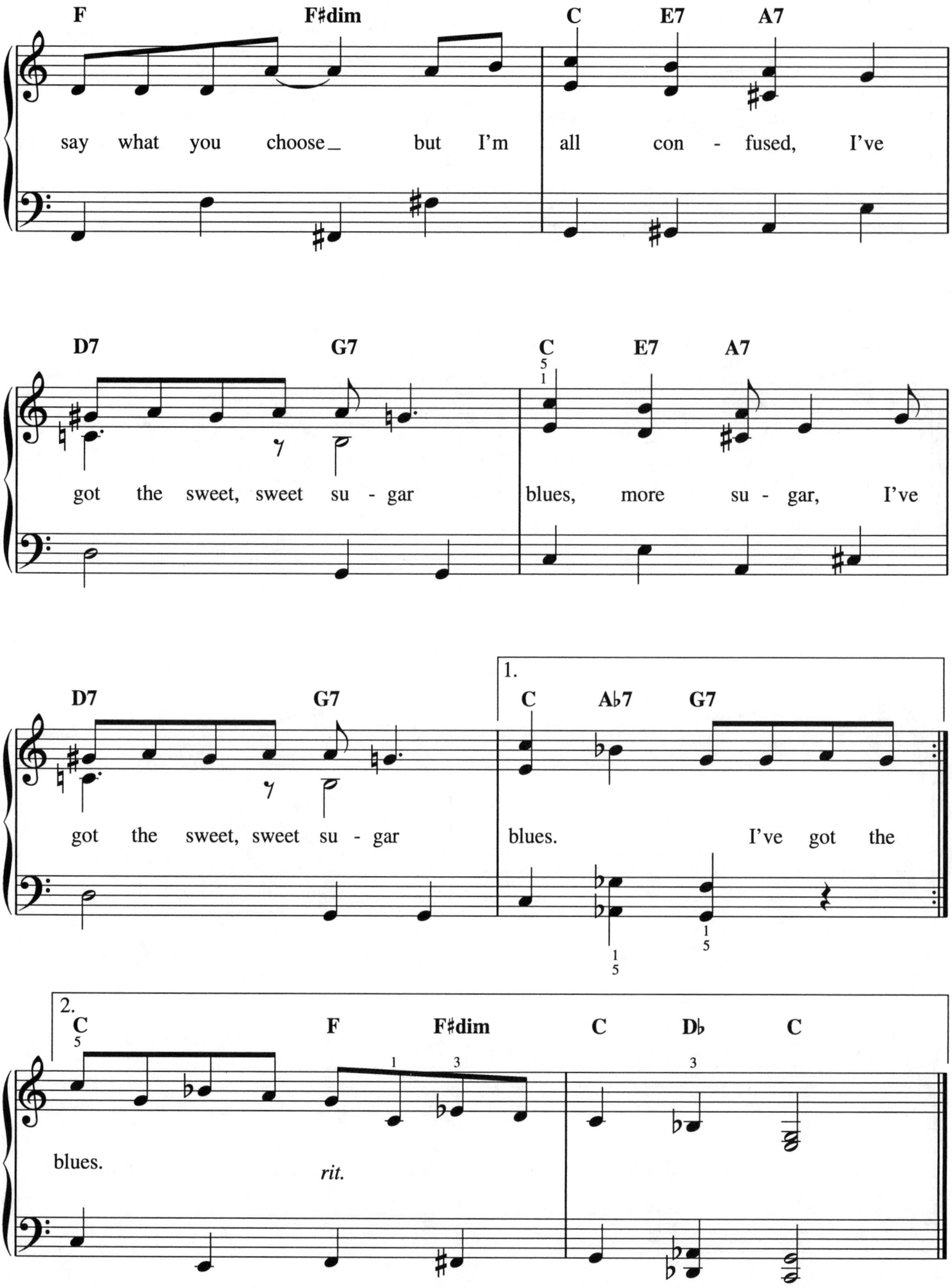
F
F♯dim
C
E7
A7
say what you choose_ but I'm all con - fused, I've
D7
G7
C
E7
A7
got the sweet, sweet su - gar blues, more su - gar, I've
D7
G7
1.
C
A♭7
G7
got the sweet, sweet su - gar blues. I've got the
2.
C
F
F♯dim
C
D♭
C
blues.
rit.

TAIN'T NOBODY'S BIZ-NESS IF I DO

Words and Music by PORTER GRAINGER
and EVERETT ROBBINS

© Copyright 1922, 1949, 1960 by MCA MUSIC PUBLISHING, A Division of MCA INC.
Copyright Renewed
International Copyright Secured All Rights Reserved
MCA music publishing

Cm
G7
Cm
But I'm gon - na do just as I want to an - y -
Of - ten times the ones that talk will get down on their
C
C7
way, and don't care if they all de -
knees and beg you par - don for their
G♭7
F7
B♭
spise me. If I should
squawk - in'. If I dis -
D7
Gm
B♭7/F
E♭
Edim7
take a no - tion to jump in to _____ the o - cean
like my lov - er and leave him for _____ an - oth - er,

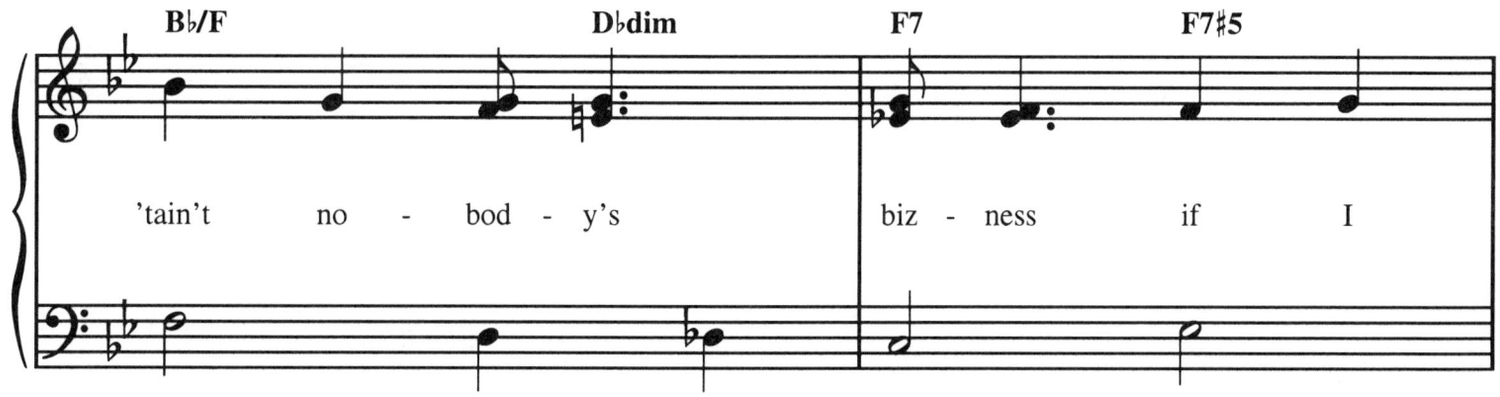
B♭/F
D♭dim
F7
F7♯5
'tain't no - bod - y's
biz - ness if I

D7♯5
G7
C9
F7♯5
B♭
do.
Rath - er than
If I go to

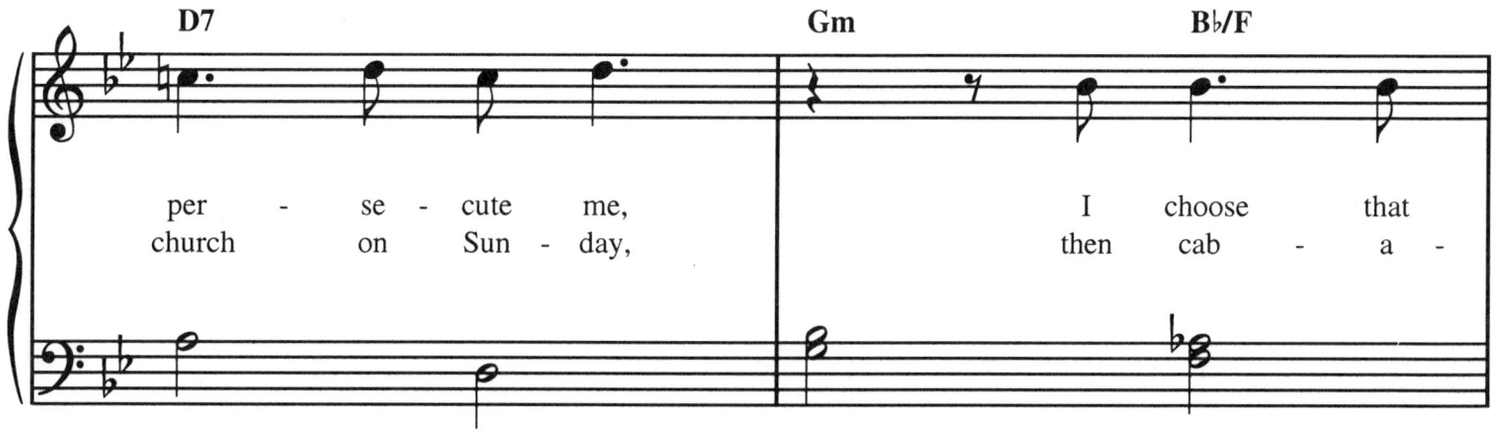
D7
Gm
B♭/F
per - se - cute me,
church on Sun - day,
I choose that
then cab - a -

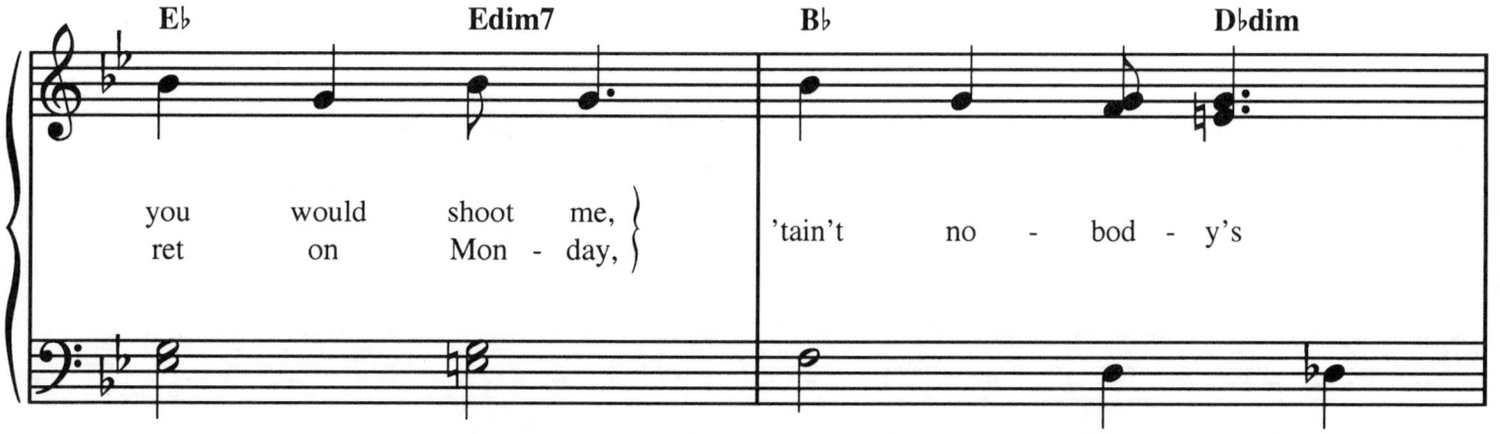
E♭
Edim7
B♭
D♭dim
you would shoot me,
ret on Mon - day,
'tain't no - bod - y's

F7
B♭
Cm7
C♯dim7
B♭/D
biz - ness if ___ I ___ do. ___

B♭
D7/A
If I should get the feel - in'
If my friend ain't got no mon - ey

Gm
B♭7/F
E♭
Edim7
to dance up - on ___ the ceil - in'
and I say, "Take all mine, hon - ey,"

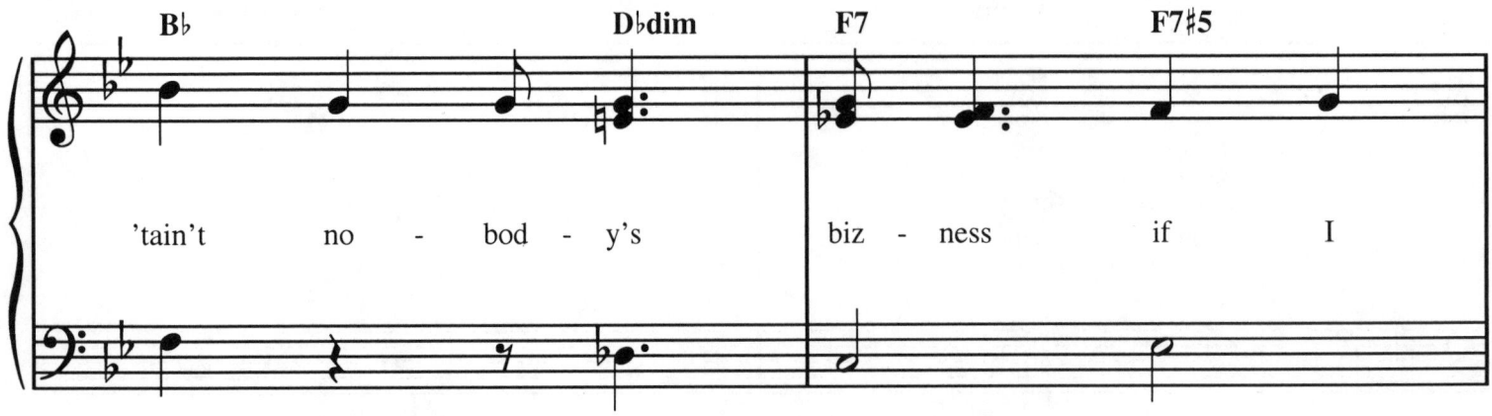
B♭
D♭dim
F7
F7♯5
'tain't no - bod - y's biz - ness if I

D7♯5 G7♭9 C9 F7♯5 B♭
do.
If I let my
If I give him
D7 Gm B♭7/F E♭ Edim7
best com - pan - ion drive me right in - to the can - yon,
my last nick - el and it leaves me in a pick - le,
B♭ D♭dim F7 F9♯5 1. B♭7 B♭dim E♭m7
'tain't no - bod - y's biz - ness if I do.
B♭ G♭9 F7 2. B♭7 E♭6 G♭7 B♭ F7♯5 B♭
do.

TOBACCO ROAD

Copyright © 1960 Cedarwood Publishing
Copyright Renewed
All Rights Administered by Songs of PolyGram International, Inc.
International Copyright Secured All Rights Reserved

Cm N.C.
in the mid - dle of To - bac - co Road. Wo wo
bring it back to To - bac - co Road. Wo wo
B♭ Cm B♭ Cm B♭
wo. Grew up in a rust - y shack,
wo. Bring dy - na - mite and a crane,
Cm B♭ Cm B♭ Cm B♭
all I had was hang - in' on my back. On - ly you know
blow it up start all o - ver a - gain. Build a town, be
Cm B♭ Cm N.C.
how I loathe this place called To - bac - co Road.
proud to show, give the name To - bac - co Road.

F7
But it's home,
But it's home,
the on - ly life I've ev - er
the on - ly life I've ev - er
C7
known.
known.
On - ly
I de -
F7 B♭ F7 B♭
you know how I loathe.
spise you 'cos you're filth - y,

F7
B♭
F7
B♭
F7
N.C.
but I
love you
To - bac - co
'cos you're home.
1.
Cm
B♭
Cm
B♭
Cm
B♭
Road.
(R.H.)
Cm
B♭
2.
Cm
A♭7
sfz
sfz
Repeat and Fade
Cm
B♭
Cm
B♭
R.H.

THE THRILL IS GONE

Words and Music by ROY HAWKINS
and RICK DARNELL

Copyright © 1951 by Powerforce Music
Copyright Renewed
All Rights Administered by Careers-BMG Music Publishing, Inc.
International Copyright Secured All Rights Reserved

G
F♯7sus
F♯7
You know you done me wrong, ba - by, and you'll be sor -
Some-day I know I'll be o-pen armed, ba - by, just like I know
Bm
F♯7
- ry some day.
a good man should.
Bm
The thrill is gone. It's gone a - way
You know I'm free, free now, ba - by. I'm free from your
from me.
spell.
Em
The thrill is gone, ba - by.
Oh, I'm free, free, free, now.

Bm
The thrill has gone a - way from me.
I'm free from your spell.
G
Al - though I'll still live on,
And now that it's all o -
F♯7
Bm
but so lone - ly I'll
ver, all I can do is wish you
1.
F♯7
be.
2.
F♯7 Bm
well.

WHY I SING THE BLUES

Words and Music by
B.B. KING

© Copyright 1969 by DUCHESS MUSIC CORPORATION and SOUNDS OF LUCILLE, INC.
All Rights Controlled and Administered by DUCHESS MUSIC CORPORATION, an MCA company
International Copyright Secured All Rights Reserved
MCA music publishing

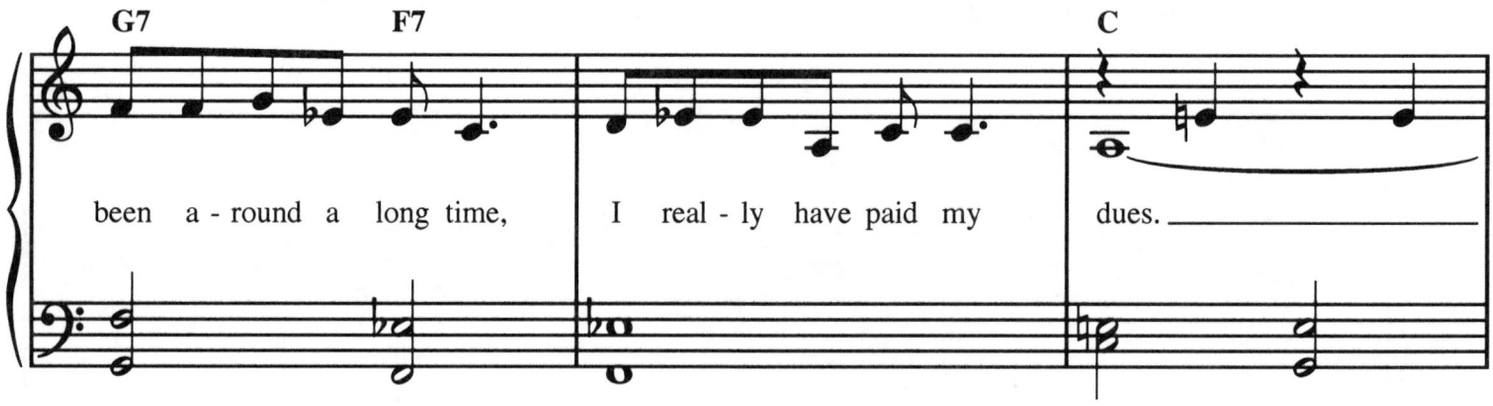
G7
F7
C
been a - round a long time,
I real - ly have paid my
dues.

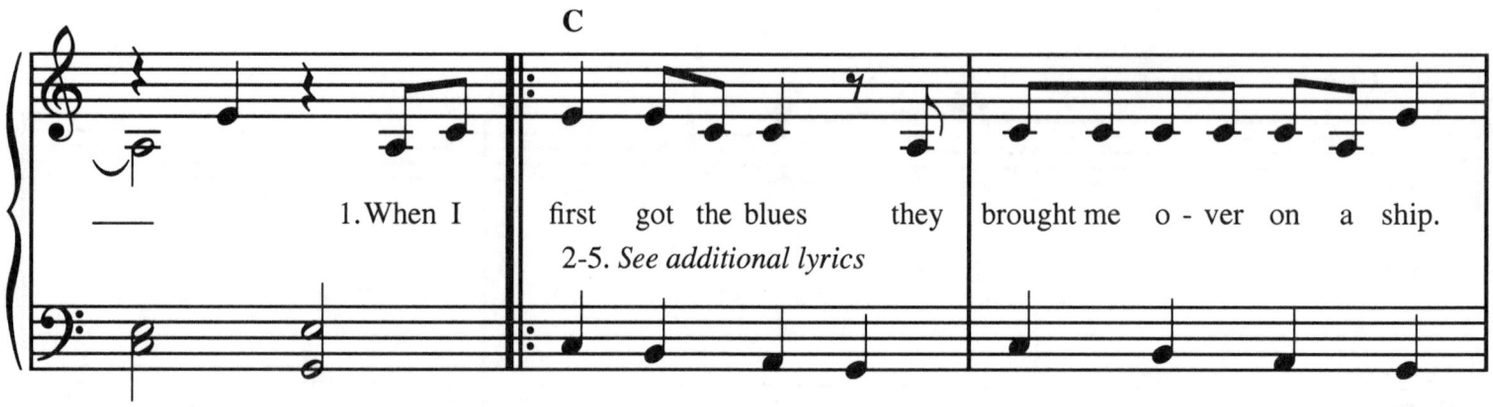
C
1. When I
first got the blues they
brought me o - ver on a ship.
2-5. See additional lyrics

3
C7
F7
Men were stand-ing o - ver me and a
lot more with the whip. And ev' - ry -
bod - y wan-na know

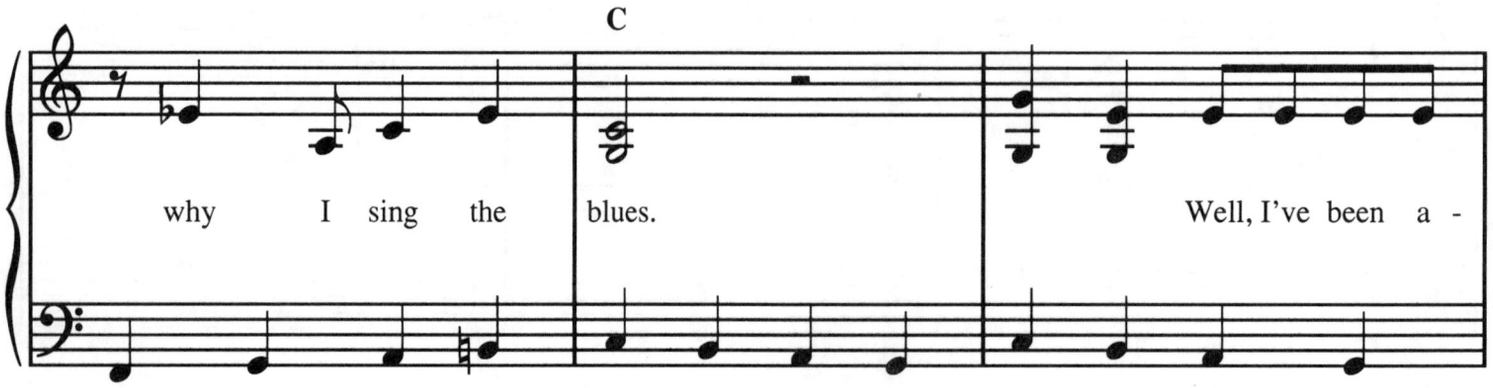
C
why I sing the
blues.
Well, I've been a -

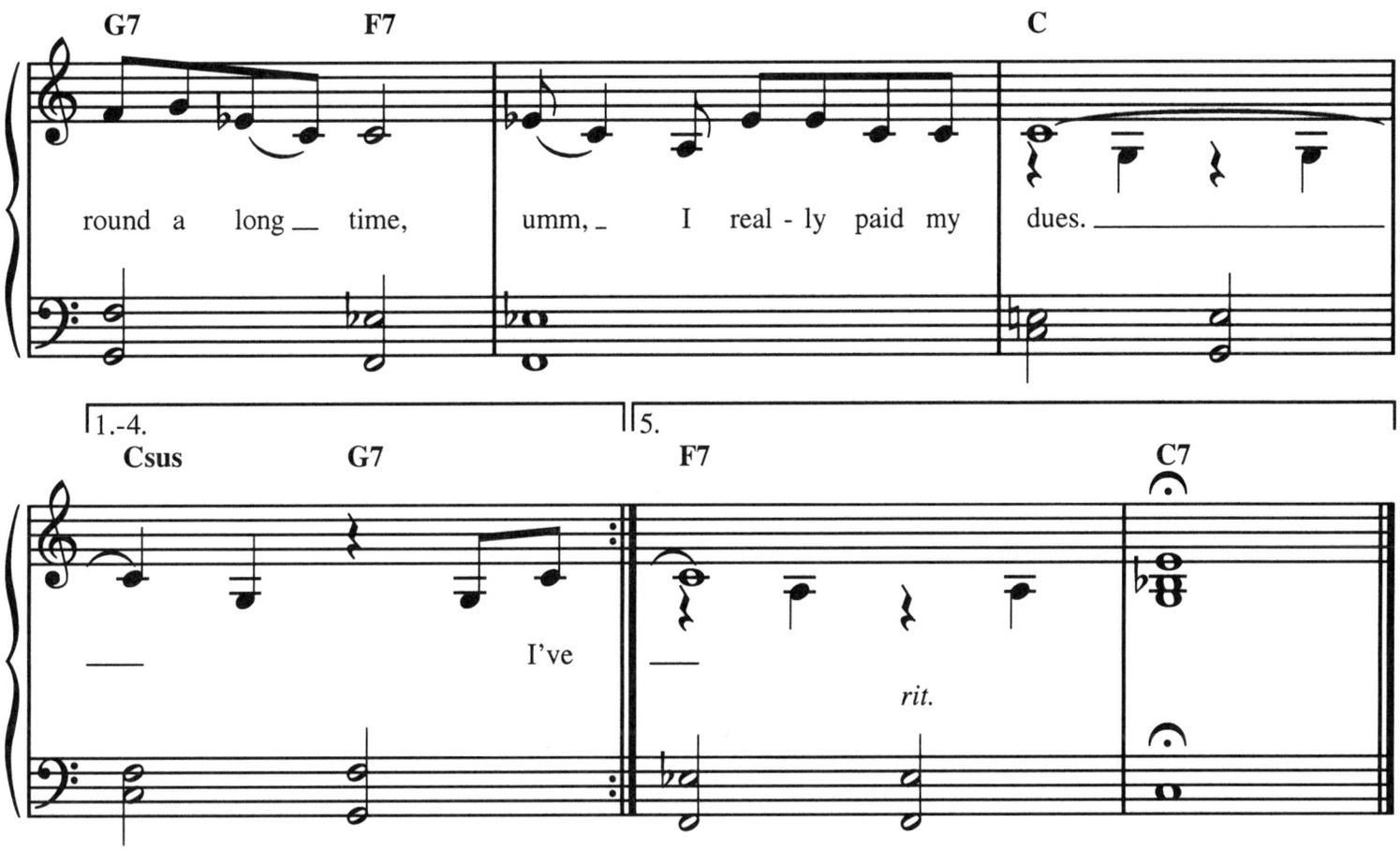

Additional Lyrics

2. I've laid in the ghetto flats, cold and numb.
   I heard the rats tell the bedbugs to give the roaches some,
   and ev'rybody wanna know why I sing the blues.
   Well I've been around a long time, Umm, I really paid my dues.

3. I stood in line down in the county hall.
   I heard a man say we are going to build some new apartments for y'all.
   (And) ev'rybody wanna know why I sing the blues.
   Well, I've been around a long time, Umm, I really paid my dues.

4. My kid's gonna grow up, gonna grow to be a fool,
   'Cause they ain't got no more room, no more for him in school.
   And everybody wants to know why I sing the blues.
   I say, I've been around a long time, yes, I've really paid my dues.

5. Yea, you know the company told me, yes, you're born to lose.
   Everybody around feel it, seems like everybody's got the blues.
   But I had them a long time, I really, really paid my dues.
   You know I ain't ashamed of it, people, I just love to sing the blues.

WEST END BLUES

Words and Music by JOE OLIVER
and CLARENCE WILLIAMS

© Copyright 1928 by MCA MUSIC PUBLISHING, A Division of MCA INC.
Copyright Renewed
International Copyright Secured All Rights Reserved
MCA music publishing

F
My bel - ly's full of gin.
I'm gon - na hear bad news.
To Coda
C7
I'm on my way to the West End, and
I'm on my
F
that's where trou - bles will be - gin.
C7
F
B♭7
My gal, my pal, low

F
F7
down, mean houn'. They're in
B♭7
town. They're cut - tin' it up. Yes, they're run - nin'
F
C7
'round. Soon I'm gon-na take a walk and
F
knock up - on her door.

C7
F
Now those
folks
in

West End,
folks
in

B♭7
West End,
they're gon - na
see
some shoot - in' like

F
they nev - er saw
be - fore.
My

C7
gal and my best pal ___ will
nev - er cheat in West End an - y -

F
C7
D. S. al Coda
more. _____
I got the

CODA
C7
way to the West End __ to
lose those _ West _ End

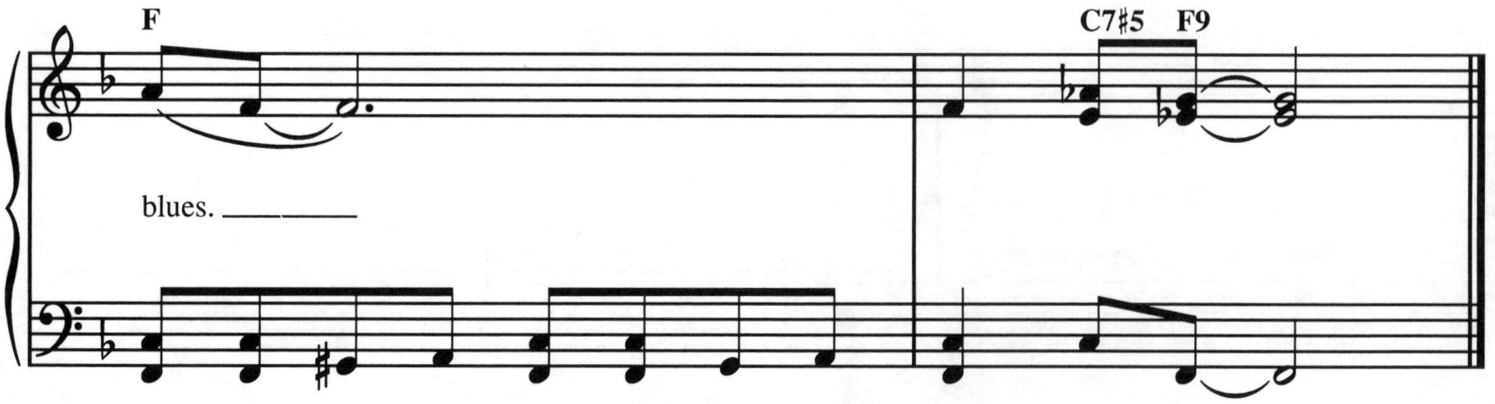
F
C7♯5
F9
blues. _____